THE WILES LECTURES
GIVEN AT THE QUEEN'S UNIVERSITY BELFAST

THE PERSONALITY OF IRELAND

The *Personality of* Ireland

HABITAT, HERITAGE AND HISTORY

E. ESTYN EVANS

EMERITUS PROFESSOR OF IRISH STUDIES
FORMERLY PROFESSOR OF GEOGRAPHY
QUEEN'S UNIVERSITY, BELFAST

CAMBRIDGE
AT THE UNIVERSITY PRESS
1973

Published by the Syndics of the Cambridge University Press
Bentley House, 200 Euston Road, London NW1 2DB
American Branch: 32 East 57th Street, New York, N.Y. 10022

© Cambridge University Press 1973

Library of Congress Catalogue Card Number: 72–83667

ISBN: 0 521 08684 1

Printed in Hong Kong by
Dai Nippon Printing Co., (Int'l) Ltd.

Contents

List of illustrations

Preface

The purpose of the Wiles Lectures, which are given annually in the Queens' University of Belfast – normally by a distinguished historian – is 'to promote the study of the history of civilisation and to encourage the extension of historical thinking into the realm of general ideas'. It may be thought presumptuous for a geographer, although by definition he is concerned with the whole wide world, to attempt to make a contribution to such a lofty theme: my excuse must be that I was invited to do so. I accepted the challenge willingly if rashly, and I wish to express my deep gratitude to Mrs J. Boyd and the Trustees of the Wiles Foundation, to Dr A. Vick, Vice-Chancellor of the University, through whom the invitation came, and to Professor M. Roberts who gave me guidance and encouragement and to whom it fell to make arrangements for the lectures under difficult circumstances. I wish also to record my gratitude to the Queen's University for facilitating my retirement, after a term of forty years, from the headship of a large department two years before my time by giving me a personal chair and transferring me to the Directorship of the newly-established Institute of Irish Studies. On my retirement in 1970, moreover, I was generously offered a Senior Fellowship in the Institute, and concurrently (1970–72) I have enjoyed a Leverhulme Emeritus Fellowship which has enabled me to travel and pursue my interests throughout Ireland and in several parts of Atlantic Europe.

In addition to colleagues from several departments of the University who attended the discussions which follow each of the four lectures, several scholars came on invitation, under the terms of the Trust, from other universities and learned institutions: Professor D. Greene, Professor Jones Hughes and Dr A.T. Lucas from Dublin; Professor E. Jones and Dr. J. Johnson from London; Professor J. Mogey from Boston (via Oxford), Professor D. Quinn from Liverpool and Mr. G. Thompson and Dr A. Gailey from the Ulster Folk Museum. I am grateful to them for their contributions to the discussions and for the helpful correspondence I have had with them since.

I have come into the historical field in a literal sense, through work in the field, and have no claim to be called an historian except in the most general sense. I have approached the subject in the spirit of Marc Bloch and Fernand Braudel, looking on cultural landscapes as having patterns which are woven into the history of man. Evangelical conservationists and anti-pollutionists are receiving so much publicity nowadays that 'environment' is coming to be narrowly conceived as the special concern of ecologists, planners and politicians. As a cultural geographer, I see it as part of human history. I have not served the exacting apprenticeship required of historical scholars, and cannot claim to have made any contribution to many of the special problems which preoccupy Irish historians. On the other hand I have ventured to explore some wider fields and have drawn freely on the findings of scholars in several related disciplines. I must ask for forgiveness if, in attempting to assess their contributions to our knowledge of the Irish cultural landscape, I have oversimplified or misinterpreted those findings. I have tried to take account, within the limits of my competence, of different sorts of evidence bearing on the history of Ireland and its peoples in the hope of demonstrating that co-operation between research workers can lead to fuller understanding.

I have expanded the lectures here and there for publication but otherwise have left them in the intentionally somewhat provocative form in which they were delivered. To the four chapters I have added as an appendix a remarkable account of agrarian conditions in County Donegal in the years before the Great Famine, first published in 1845.

I wish to offer my thanks to the following for their help in selecting and preparing the illustrations and in other ways: Dr R. Common, Miss E. Duncan, Mr D. Evans, Mr W.F. Little, Dr D. McCourt, Mr N.C. Mitchel, Dr J.K. St Joseph and Mr J. Bambury; and to Mr P.L. Henry and Mrs M. Kennedy for bibliographical assistance.

The Institute of Irish Studies   E. Estyn Evans
Queen's University   10 February 1972
Belfast

I

Habitat, heritage and history

an anthropogeographic view

I have been given the opportunity and the privilege of presenting to historians, and particularly to Irish historians, some thoughts on – and some illustrations of – the relationships between geography and history. I am well aware that my brand of anthropogeography, which is that of H.J. Fleure and Carl O. Sauer, is currently out of fashion, and that a preoccupation with relevance and prediction, and recently with perception and the behavioural environment, has led to a drift away from a genetic approach to human geography, and from historical explanation. Most of my geographical colleagues would say that the pressing problems of the modern world are more than enough to occupy them, and that history can be trusted to look after the past. Leaving aside the difficulty of deciding when the present becomes the past, and leaving aside also the question whether, in modern Western society, history need be a guide to action, study of the past cannot but give perspective, and the wider and deeper the perspective the better our understanding of the present. My concern is with environment as a factor in human history, and although I might have wished that someone better versed in recent methodological developments had been chosen to present the claims of my subject to historical scholars, it must be admitted that the current passion for enumeration tends to restrict the interests of the younger generation to a short time span. Quantification, because of an inevitable lack of data, can give only a limited understanding of the past, nor can it be applied to some of the most precious ingredients of civilisation.

Looking at one of the most heroic attempts to reach what I take to be the ultimate goal of history – that is, universal human history – even a young geographer could find abundant material to patch some of the environmental holes in the majestic canvas of Toynbee's work, *A Study of History*. His most perceptive geographical critic, O.H.K. Spate, regards Toynbee's understanding and handling of geography as the weakest part of his study. The anthropologist, too, takes exception to his arbitrary selection of twenty-one societies, past and present, as exemplars of civilisation, leaving out of the reckoning, as the concern of anthropologists, 'over 650' other human societies. Toynbee apparently took his figure of 650 from Professor Hobhouse, although Professor Leyburn had estimated the number of world societies at over 12,000. This is anyhow a false dichotomy. Even supposing that the anthropologist is concerned only with primitive societies, where are we to draw the line? Most modern

1

societies have a 'primitive' as well as a 'civilised' side, and heritage, or unrecorded history, is an essential part of all cultures. Moreover, by treating his twenty-one civilisations as isolates, Toynbee minimises the significance of diffusion.

In dismissing environmental determinism, only to substitute his own brand, which Spate sums up as 'the determinism of relatively unfavourable environments', Toynbee makes easy game of such recent advocates of climatic control as Ellsworth Huntington. But he turns more readily to the ancient world – for theories of environmental causation have a respectable classical ancestry – and many of the views he so readily demolishes are taken from Greek and Roman writers. This is an extreme illustration of a risk all would-be synthesisers face: the reliance on out-moded and often secondary authority when working in fields other than their own. But they must also face prejudice in venturing to tread on territory which carries the property mark of other academic disciplines. Toynbee was attacked by the learned on almost all sides, and his ex-perience suggests that – if I may malappropriate a No Trespass notice I once saw in an American wood-lot – 'Survivors will be persecuted'. Another fate may await lesser mortals who dare to trespass, and that is to be watched by those on the other side of the fence with an air of detachment and indifference.

The theme I have chosen, however, calls for many border forays or rather let me say for trans-border co-operation. I am pleading the cause of a trilogy of regional studies, of habitat, heritage and history: that is of geography, anthropology (in its widest sense, including the behavioural sciences, as well as prehistory) and recorded history (including social and economic history). I take the view that all these subjects can be regarded as parts of human history, as various approaches to the study of the evolution of man and society on this earth. Of course they all have their own objectives, and I am suggesting that they should interpenetrate rather than amalgamate. Even assuming that it were practicable to make a combined subject for educational purposes, on the model of some approaches to undergraduate studies in the humanities, I believe more would be lost than gained if academics were to be drawn away from their specialist fields, but they should be aware of what is going on beyond the fence: it is at the fences, along the borders, that discoveries are likely to be made. In such broad fields of study, wrote Julian Huxley, discussing not the past but the future of man, 'we must envisage networks of co-operative investigation . . . the social sciences as a whole cannot escape the pressure towards integration',[1] and he makes a plea for a common terminology and an end to technical jargon. Certainly some of the mistrust and misunderstanding of the other fellow's subject arises from the fashion of using terms which bring obfuscation rather than clarification. One suspects that these specialist vocabularies are sometimes designed to win academic respectability rather than to facilitate communication. I shall shun them.

By habitat I mean the total physical environment, and by history the written record of the past. I would define heritage in broad terms as the unwritten segment of human history, comprising man's physical, mental, social and cultural inheritance from a prehistoric past, his oral traditions, beliefs, languages, arts and crafts. It seems to me that there is no ideological gap between anthropology and conventional history in so far as they are concerned with the human experience. Lévi-Strauss regards them as 'indissociables'. Many anthropologists, however, have been hostile to history, partly no doubt because of the extravagances committed by the so-called historical school of anthropology. The functional anthropologists in particular have been critical of historical reconstructions and conjectural history. Since anyhow British anthropology has been primarily concerned with 'primitives' and British academic history with the peoples of Britain and Europe there has been little common ground. Anthropologists, however, are increasingly busying themselves with European communities and with the peasant peoples whose 'little tradition' persists alongside the 'great tradition' of the élites which has provided the stuff of recorded history. Moreover, the collection of popular traditions, oral literature and folk customs which was part of the Romantic movement has been transformed and systematised under the inspiration of Scandinavian scholars into the academic discipline of ethnology or folklife, enriching and illuminating the content of recorded history. The folk movement, too, is part of history in another sense, for it inspired nationalist revivals in many European countries, not least in Ireland through the Anglo-Irish literary movement and the Gaelic League. Already in late eighteenth-century Belfast, the United Irishmen, mainly Presbyterians, were steeped in Irish tradition, folk music and antiquarianism; and 'the idea of an "Irish nation", indifferent to religious rivalries, rooted in history . . . takes its rise in the Belfast of the late eighteenth century'.[2] But while folklife as an academic discipline has long been recognised in Scandinavian countries, Ireland has had to wait until 1971 to see the first Department of Folklore established, in University College, Dublin.

Prehistoric studies won academic status much earlier, even in Ireland, having passed from the Romantic phase of antiquarian exploration to the stage of scientific classification and excavation in the course of last century, primarily in Denmark and England. The prehistoric time-scale overlaps with the historic, for the mass of the world's population has remained non-literate down to recent times. Many academic historians, however, still attach little importance to archaeological evidence, even when it relates to historic periods, and accord to it at best a subsidiary role, ignoring or disbelieving the view expressed so long ago as 1881 by J.R. Green: 'archaeological researches yield evidence even more trustworthy than that

3

of written chronicle, while the ground itself . . . is the fullest and the most certain of documents'.[3]

Green, we may notice, found geography an equally indispensible aid to history and felt that, to give an adequate account of Anglo-Saxon settlement, he was obliged to consider and map the distribution of marsh and woodland in lowland England. His views on the relevance and usefulness of these sources were exceptional. Into the present century, wrote R.G. Collingwood, 'it was felt that unwritten sources of history could give valid results only on a very small scale and when they were used as an auxiliary arm to "written sources"; and only about low matters like industry and commerce, into which an historian with the instincts of a gentleman would not enquire'.[4] In Ireland, according to George Petrie, there had once been even more prejudice: not only the antiquities but also the history of the country previous to the Anglo-Norman invasion 'were considered to be involved in obscurity and darkness such as no sane mind would venture to penetrate'.[5] In recent years, with the refinements of palaeobotanical techniques and radio-carbon dating (C14, which historians have been known to take as a reference to the fourteenth century), prehistory has acquired a chronological scale of considerable depth and accuracy to guide and inspire excavation; and the reconstruction of many aspects of the economy, material culture, art, settlement forms and burial rituals of successive periods is now a commonplace of excavation reports. If archaeology can make no claim to obtain information on human thought and emotions, save inferentially, herein, for some enthusiasts, lies its advantage over written history. When conventional history takes over, the prehistorian Harold Peake used to say, the story gets blurred by the prejudices of men who write it.

Geography has now won almost universal recognition in the universities, though characteristically Ireland came late in the field, and if its methodology is constantly changing, its broad concern – the areal differentiation of the world and its peoples – has been a matter of enquiry and speculation since classical Greek times. Its immemorial symbol is the map, but although geographers like to have their fingers on the map and their feet on the ground, they cannot but be aware of philosophical aspects of their subject, of the mystery as well as the reality of man's place in nature. Geography was described by the pioneer American conservationist, G.P. Marsh, as both a poetry and a philosophy. Anthropology has not yet found a place in the universities of the Irish Republic, but after long advocacy of their kinship with geography, both anthropology and archaeology have chairs at Queen's University, Belfast. It is part of my purpose to show how history can profitably co-operate with these sister subjects in regional research. We who practise these relatively new academic disciplines should remind ourselves that historians, economists and other social scientists have also had to fight for the general admission of their subjects into British universities, and that less than fifty years have passed since Professor Tout could claim that the battle for the recognition of history was as good as won.

The serious professional study of Irish history, one of its practitioners has recently said, is barely a generation old, and much of its scholarly output relates to the activities of politicians, many of them English. Until recent times, indeed, writers of what was termed 'Irish history' seem to have been preoccupied with the morbid phenomena of British rule in their country: '1169 and all that' done into academic prose. I have found this kind of history confusing and repellent, a record of violence and corruption if sometimes of heroism and vision, and it is an irrelevancy that some of the personalities involved, we are told, hated the corruption they were forced to practise. I have wondered whether Lord Acton could have had this sort of Irish history in mind when he said, as has been reported, that he was turned to gloom by the contemplation of the affairs of men. But I am not a trained historian. I took a course of history at the University College of Wales nearly half a century ago, but found it so myopic in its insular view of the world – even though the course was regarded as an enlightened innovation, however inappropriate in a Welsh College, called Colonial History – that it was a relief to turn to geography and to be plunged forthwith, by H.J. Fleure, into the loess and the cultures of north China in the company of Ferdinand von Richthofen. Academic history, it seems, was slow to break away from the view of Bishop Stubbs that history meant the history of the British parliament and constitution. No doubt there are some Englishmen who would defend this definition, but Professor Gordon Childe, an Australian, was reacting strongly against such an interpretation, as well as against the theological model of history, when he brought his book *What Happened in History* (1942) to an abrupt end with the spread of Christianity in the ancient Mediterranean world. One could wish that he had given us a new Childe's History of England.[6]

No prehistorian did more in his time than Childe to extend the scope of history, to make it the history of man on earth, the scientific study of all sources of information on the human past. A prehistorian and a geographer, H.J.E. Peake and H.J. Fleure, made a similar approach in *The Corridors of Time* (1927–56), and Professor Grahame Clark has been for many years a leading exponent of world prehistory. Because of the limitations of the evidence, those prehistorians who have looked for uniformities – they hesitate to call them laws – have tended to lean towards environmental or cultural determinism. Deprived of any knowledge of the creative spirit of prehistoric personalities, they have not subscribed to the Great Man theory of history, and have been more concerned with processes than events. On the whole, the conceptual framework of archaeologists has been technological or ecological, though few go so far

5

as to claim that these factors controlled institutions and beliefs. Childe's near-Marxist insistence on the significance of technological and economic change contrasts with the comparative neglect of material culture in many anthropological studies of modern primitives. Thus Evans-Pritchard, in his celebrated work on the Nuer, deals fully with social life and political institutions but remarks that he is 'neither desirous nor capable of describing technological procedures'.[7] Those anthropologists, however, who see material culture and technology as an objective test of the degree of civilisation, linked with mental aptitudes and social development, point out moreover that language must have referred to concrete things before it could be extended into the realms of ideas and ethics. Improved technology and associated ideas must enlarge vocabulary and lead to linguistic modification. Language change in prehistoric times, which seems to have been not infrequent before languages became firmly enshrined in religious phrases and tied to localities among sedentary communities, would probably have been facilitated and speeded by technological innovation. This has a possible bearing, as we shall point out, on the vexed question of the spread of the Celtic tongue in Ireland.

Here I would put in a plea for the inclusion in our general academic system of training in the use of manual and visual skills. An obsession with book-learning has tended to divorce education from reality and led teachers to disregard or even despise the educational content of the cultural environment; and nowhere is this more evident than in scholastic Ireland. It is true that school education has come to include instruction in the experimental verification of scientific method, but field observation is relatively undeveloped as a tool for cultivating an awareness of the cultural heritage. A practical knowledge of simple technology would not only provide young people with a creative environmental link, but give them also a sympathetic understanding of the human past and of the 'primitive' folk of the contemporary world. I have always found it an advantage, in studying rural life in Ireland, to participate in any agricultural or craft process I wished to understand and describe, and it will be remembered that the French agrarian historian, Marc Bloch, wrote his classic books as a farmer who could plough, who knew the feel of the land and the smell of hay and manure. He was able to look beyond the legal and institutional framework of agrarian systems, interpreting them on the ground and in the intimacy of small regions. In much the same way I have tried to read the rural landscape and have come to see it as the key to the continuity of Irish history.

It is on climatological grounds that environmental determinism has been most strongly argued by geographers and others. Scandinavian archaeologists in particular have been wedded to the idea of climatic change as a potent factor in human destiny, and their pioneer palaeobotanical researches, relating vegetational and cultural change to climatic deterioration, seemed to confirm, for example, the native legends of *Fimbulwinter*. There seem to be instances, in critically marginal climatic environments such as Greenland, where climatic oscillations and their vegetational responses have had dramatic consequences, but as we shall see, some prehistoric vegetational changes as revealed by pollen studies can plausibly be interpreted in terms of man's interference with the balance of vegetation. The influence of climate on man and his societies has been a matter for speculation since classical times, and interest in the topic has by no means been confined to geographers. One recalls the famous dictum of Montesquieu: 'the empire of the climate is the first, the most powerful, of all empires'. It was the thesis of Ellsworth Huntington that great civilisations have been located in regions enjoying climates which he thought favourable; and he made climatic oscillation the prime mover of nomads in his imaginative work, *The Pulse of Asia*, (1907). But there is no end to climatic correlations. Of the many inane examples given by various authors I need cite only the uncomfortable conclusion of S.F. Markham, that 'up to the 15th century, every Jew of importance was born on or near the 70°(F) isotherm'.[8] Single-factor causation is rarely proved, and climate, however dramatically it may display its forces, is but one element of the total environment of man. To isolate it is not only, in the words of Vidal de la Blache, 'morceler ce que la nature rassemble', but also to ignore the cultural heritage of the society it is supposed to control.

Among those scholars who, lacking a geographical training, came to insist on the significance of general environmental influences on the development of regional cultures I must single out the archaeologist, Sir Cyril Fox, whose monograph *The Personality of Britain* (1932) – probably the best-known work bearing the title I have chosen for these lectures – is sub-titled: 'Its influence on inhabitant and invader in prehistoric and early historic times'. Its influence was certainly marked on a whole generation of archaeologists. Fox made no less than twenty-five 'propositions' relating to environmental influences, but his main thesis was that lowland Britain has been characterised by cultural replacement and unity, highland Britain by cultural absorption and continuity. The division of Britain into highland and lowland zones, along a line running approximately from Teesmouth to Exmouth, had been made earlier by Sir Halford Mackinder, though Fox was apparently unaware of Mackinder's analysis of positional geography. General correlations between archaeological distributions and types of environment had also been made by the German Robert Gradmann, and this line of enquiry was taken up in Britain by H.J. Fleure and O.G.S. Crawford, but as geographers they were more aware of the complexities of man/nature relationships. Fleure, in particular, would add an Atlantic zone and would see the zone of contact between highland and lowland as of critical importance, instancing the prominence of Salisbury Plain as a meeting place of early cultures. While personality for Fox meant the total physical environment – he did not, for example, isolate a particular element such as climate – his argument is simplified and falsified by the concept of environment as a given phenomenon, waiting, as it were, for its human conquerors or victims. For the human or cultural geographer, environment without man is not environment: both are abstractions unless they are taken together. This is the core of traditional human geography as exposed and expounded by the founder-fathers, Alexander von Humboldt (1769–1859) and Karl Ritter (1779–1859), and later clarified by the findings of Charles Darwin, whose *Origin of Species* appeared in the year in which both Humboldt and Ritter died.

Taking a broad view of the world and its peoples, it is clear that different varieties of the human race, with different societal forms and goals, are associated with different environments, for example Europe, south-east Asia or tropical Africa. These diversities have given rise to much ingenious speculation from time to time, and some of the world's oldest myths pretend to explain, for instance, why some peoples are light-skinned and others dark-skinned. In Europe, speculation on such problems was particularly active in the Renaissance and in the eighteenth century, stimulated in the first place by the startling revelations of the voyages of discovery and later by the rational questioning of scriptural authority. Consideration of the nature and distribution of these geographical diversities inevitably led to discussion of the time-dimension, and what concerns us here is that it was in Ireland that a precise biblical time-scale was worked out by Archbishop Ussher in 1650. His theochronology, beginning with the creation of the world in 4004 B.C., has had a profound influence on our educational system and may be said to have delayed the full acceptance of a scientific view of the evolution of man and society. It illustrates Ireland's reverence for traditional Christian beliefs – for a view of man as a being outside nature – as well as the ingenuity with which many Irishmen have justified these beliefs.

The conception of the former purity and uniformity, physical and cultural, of created man lies behind persistent theories of an original purity of race or of cultural features such as language. These theories have taken many forms. Hyperdiffusionism, as preached with evangelical fervour by Elliot Smith and W.J. Perry, has been described as a scientific variation on the biblical theme of the scattering from the Tower of Babel, and this version met the international mood of the first half of the nineteenth century. According to Perry, for example, all funerary monuments in stone represent a single cultural influence; and the extreme diffusionist view was that all great discoveries have taken place once and once only. The corollary was that, without diffusion, there must be cultural retrogression. Lord Raglan, an aristocratic advocate of diffusion, sees the scholar's rejection of his views as an unwillingness 'to abandon their pretence to a localized omniscience'. He is more to the point when he observes that 'the theory of diffusion is anathema to all nationalists'.[9] For, though the alternative simplistic theory of cultural growth in parallel, evolving through stages at varying rates but in a fixed unilinear sequence (the so-called comparative or 'psychic unity' theory), is at least as old as Vitruvius, it was encouraged by the growth of nationalism and religious schism in the sixteenth century. National pride in supposedly indigenous culture, however, was strangely at variance with the manifest diffusion of Christianity; and this may be one of the reasons why, in Ireland, the Roman Catholic hierarchy was a reluctant supporter of nationalism.

A ferment of ideas on the relationships between environment and customs and morals was stirring in the thought of eighteenth century Europe and some of the concepts then reaching the surface have outlived Darwinism. They have recently been admirably discussed by a geographer in a work sub-titled 'Nature and Culture in Western Thought to 1800'.[10] It may be said that both environmentalism and the fixed stage theory tended to regard environment as a separate static force and to ignore culture contact. While it will be admitted that the environment must have some bearing on human cultures, its physical nature and the resources it provides cannot by themselves explain anything. For the cultural geographer, as I have said, environment taken by itself is an abstraction. Societies are constantly altering their environments. One of the great contributions of scholars such as Childe and Fleure was to see diffusion, not as an occasional inspired happening, but as a universal process bringing change through culture-contact and, so long as there is no great disparity of cultural levels, stimulating innovation through the cross fertilisation of ideas. The geographer and the anthropologist cannot regard invading armies, rulers, statesmen or other Great Men as the chief makers of history, or great literatures as the sole test of culture.

Since many of the world's societies have little or no recorded history, and since, even in Europe, the bulk of the population has found little or no place therein, it follows that, for an understanding of human history in any region, something more than documentary history is required. We must take account, so far as we can discover it, of the unwritten parts of cultural history; and it is the conviction of the human geographer that the land itself is much more than a location for events but is bound up with the nature of those events and with the nature of the society it supports. We come back to habitat, heritage and history. In making this three-way approach to the study of regional personality I am following the example of French historians and geographers. I was introduced to it by H.J. Fleure, a Channel Islander, who published in 1918 an address entitled *The Trilogy of the humanities in education*. It was given, with a characteristic modesty which may be both admired and deplored, to the

Tredegar and District Co-operative Society.[11] In it he pleaded for the study of human experience, chorologically, chronologically and typologically, through the disciplines of place, time and type. 'Geography, history and anthropology', he wrote, 'are a trilogy to be broken only with severe loss of truth'. Extreme environmentalists and hyperdiffusionists have tended to select their examples indiscriminately and to disregard the trilogy. Given these three variables, the search for general laws governing cultural growth is likely to discover only laws which are so general as to be of little value. Fleure thought it more important to try to understand a case deeply than to look for general laws. His broad training in the natural sciences and its application to human history are well illustrated in the ten volumes of *The Corridors of Time*, and in his last work, recently revised, on *The Natural History of Man in Britain*.

The acknowledged French master of a combined human geography and history was P. Vidal de la Blache (1845–1918), Professor of Geography in the University of Paris, and through the teaching of a succession of gifted geographers French historians have generally been fully conscious of environmental relations. As an Irish historian, Professor David Quinn, has said, 'The good old-fashioned historical geography which was drummed into French historians made them realize that oceans and mountains and climates and vegetations were often more significant in laying bases for societal forms and attitudes than political postures or intellectual constructs about hierarchy in human society.'[12] Vidal's *Tableau de la Géographie de la France* (1911) formed the first volume of E. Lavisse's *Histoire de France*. Its first section was entitled 'Personnalité géographique de la France', and it was from the use of the term by Vidal de la Blache that the concept of regional personality became one of the central themes in human geography between about 1920 and 1950, when it went out of favour. One of its most frequent users has been Jean Gottmann, now Professor of Geography in the University of Oxford. Vidal himself had adopted the word as early as 1888, and he appears to have borrowed it from the greatest of French Romantic historians, Jules Michelet, whose *Histoire de France* appeared in 1833. Some writers have preferred the word 'individuality' to 'personality', but I have retained it in homage to my French masters.[13]

French historians such as Marc Bloch, Lucien Febvre, and their disciple Fernand Braudel have amply demonstrated in their writings the rewards of a broadly geographical approach to history. Febvre pleads for the co-operation of geographers, historians and 'even sociologists' in investigating problems of society and environment.[14] Braudel begins his study of the Mediterranean world in the sixteenth century with a moving panorama of the Great Sea and its space relations. And he must look into the heritage of transhumance, for as he says, 'the history of mountain areas is that they have no history'. For him geography is not so much an introduction to history as an integral part of it. 'Did not the flowers re-appear every spring?' he asks.[15] I would see this French genius for synthesis as itself an example of regional personality, for it has been one of the roles of a land which is at the cross-roads of Western Europe – and particularly of that metropolitan cradle, the Paris Basin – not only to turn ideas into revolutions but to weave together strands of art and learning derived from all parts of the continent and to produce for the benefit of the civilised world shining novelties of many kinds. Similarly one might suggest that the dominant interest and aptitudes of English historians (or geographers or archaeologists) reflect the personality of England; and it is perhaps fair to say that German scholars, in contrast to both English and French, have a passion for specialisation and for definitions and classifications.

At this point I should like to give an example of the French gift of synthesis by summarising a recent study of the origin and diffusion of the sheep dog made by Xavier de Planhol, Professor of Geography in the University of Paris.[16] It is a topic not so remote as might appear from my central subject, the Personality of Ireland, for it touches on the history of pastoral society and on the decline of breeds of dog such as the wolf hound, for which Ireland was once famed. Not all the conclusions reached in this study may stand the test of time, but the way in which the argument as to the origin of the sheep dog is developed demonstrates clearly the value of combining historical, cultural and environmental data.

Although the dog appears to be the oldest and most widely distributed of all man's domesticated animals, the sheep dog or herding dog is a cultural element that was peculiar to Western Europe until it was diffused thence to the overseas colonies. It has been assumed that the herding dog is of great antiquity but it is not recorded before the fifteenth century in the British Isles (presumed older breeds such as the Welsh corgi should perhaps be regarded as yard dogs rather than as true herding dogs). Its adoption on the European mainland took place mainly in the eighteenth century, and it did not penetrate into Russia, where as we know wolves have been a great menace and where flocks are controlled and safeguarded in other ways. It seems that it was only when wolves were exterminated or at least greatly reduced in numbers that herding dogs gained a foothold in Europe, replacing guard dogs such as the mastiff and the wolf hound whose function was to protect flocks and herds. The guard dogs were supplemented in various ways: by pastoral pipe music – or whistles or the blast of horns – by the judicious use of clods of earth or sling stones (perhaps used for this pastoral purpose before they became weapons of war) or by including goats in the herds to act as more sensitive and intelligent guides. This may be offered as an explanation, though many other reasons have been suggested, for the belief still found in parts of the British Isles that it is lucky to include a goat

11

with a herd of cows. The powerful guard dog is typical of the wild steppes and mountains of Central Asia, while the herding dog goes with the strongly humanised landscapes of Western Europe. The adoption of the herding dog, says de Planhol, coincided not only with the diminishing threat of wolves but with a period of increasing population and a more intensive land utilisation; and these well-trained animals were particularly useful in openfield country where a variety of new crops ripening at different times of the year was coming to be cultivated on the still unenclosed arable strips. He points out that such openfield landscapes needed, and produced, the best shepherds and the best-trained sheep dogs. In long-enclosed country such as the Mediterranean lands and parts of Atlantic Europe there was less need for herding dogs; and they reached south Spain and Crete, for example, only in the present century.

In most parts of the British Isles herding dogs replaced guard dogs from the fifteenth century onwards, with the effective reduction of the wolf population, but de Planhol finds that they are recorded in Iceland as far back as the thirteenth century and were thence, it seems, diffused over Western Europe in the wake of the wolf. But why Iceland? Here we come to the environmental factor. This remote and geologically youthful island, with its restricted flora and fauna, is the only part of Europe which has never had wolves or other large predators, so that dogs could safely be bred for docility and productive use as herders. De Planhol's thesis opens up other lines of enquiry: for instance the adoption of herding dogs in the British Isles may have led to a reduction of man-power and to larger flocks and herds, and may thus have a bearing on the expansion of pastoral economies. These are lines of enquiry that de Planhol has not pursued, but what he has done is to reveal, by combining geography, history and cultural anthropology, an innovative response that can be set alongside the flowering, in the same harsh environment, of the political and literary genius of the Scandinavian people who had absorbed there, we may observe in passing, a considerable Irish heritage.

British historical geographers have tended to work within a more restricted framework and have been concerned not so much with the part played by environment in the course of history as with the reconstruction of past geographies and with functional inter-relationships at given periods. Using documentary materials supplemented by maps, place-name evidence and observation in the field, geographers such as Professor H.C. Darby have in this way made a distinctive and scholarly contribution to knowledge. In addition to such static cross sections of cultural landscapes, however, there have been many thematic studies by historical geographers of the history of particular environmental elements such as climate, woodlands, field-systems and settlements. I may cite the researches of Glanville Jones, who has used historical and archaeological data to elucidate and portray in map form the structure and development of rural settlement in early medieval Celtic Britain. Geographers and archaeologists have also collaborated with economic historians in investigating the lost villages of England, a rewarding enterprise associated particularly with the name of Maurice Beresford, though there are several other distinguished contributors. In France, Braudel has played a characteristic part as synthesist in the same field.[17]

In Ireland, we have been faced with special difficulties in linking geographical and historical studies. In the universities, geography was sponsored by geology, not by history, and while geography began with a physical bias, history has tended to lean towards politics and institutions and the study of individuals rather than of human society. This preoccupation with the élites, and with what has been termed 'battle-history', is partly explained by the relative paucity of documentary material on other aspects of Irish history, but partly, I suggest, by what I am calling the personality of the island. In the enormous collections of pamphlets – estimated at about 100,000 – which constitute one of the main sources for the eighteenth and nineteenth centuries, three themes are dominant: political relations between England and Ireland, economic distress, and religious cleavage. The social history of the country before the eighteenth century has hardly been touched by modern scholarship, and thanks to intensive archaeological field-work we probably have more firm facts about the conditions of life in the Neolithic period than in medieval Gaelic Ireland. Much of the raw material of Irish social history lies in the oral traditions of country folk. Professor K.H. Connell is drawing on this, through the great collections of the Irish Folklore Commission, to supplement and extend his pioneer work, which was based on printed sources, on the population of Ireland during the century following 1750.[18] Concentration on precisely dated sources for a set period and the neglect of what took place in other times and places give his first book both its strength and its weakness. For earlier periods the scarcity of documentary evidence, whether in English or Gaelic, for the condition of the peasantry is a limiting factor. The abundant but unevenly explored material in the old Irish literature appears to be even more narrowly concerned with the upper strata of the population than that relating to Anglo-Norman Ireland. Cattle folk, anyhow, have less need of records than arable husbandmen; nor has the habit of incendiarism favoured the preservation of records.

For their part, historical geographers and archaeologists have tried in recent years to fill some of the gaps by field study, distributional mapping and excavation; and as an example of a geographer's contributions I would cite the investigations of Dr R.E. Glasscock on moated habitation sites in medieval Ireland.[19] Through field survey and the study of old maps and new air photographs, supplemented by selective excavation, he has identified several hundred probable examples of a type of rural settlement which has been almost entirely overlooked by historians but which provides important evidence concerning rural settlement and social conditions in medieval Ireland. Moated sites are widely but unevenly distributed through the lowlands of the southern half of the country, clustering thickly in certain border areas such as east Cork. Geographical distribution in itself raises questions as to other forms of settlement in Anglo-Norman Ireland, and Dr Glasscock has turned his attention to the problem of deserted medieval boroughs and villages and has joined forces with the distinguished historian of Anglo-Norman Ireland, Professor J. Otway-Ruthven, in this promising enterprise. Further, he has recently organised a Group for the Study of Irish Historic Settlement which has already held productive meetings in various parts of the country, attended by geographers, historians, archaeologists, students of folklife and other academics as well as by local historians and field workers. This co-operative endeavour is a promising breach in the defences which have kept our various academic disciplines apart.

It must be admitted that Irish historians have had little regard for environmental studies. They have been more document-bound than most historians. I have said that their preoccupation with the élites, with parliamentary procedures and political personalities, might be regarded as a reflection of the personality of the island itself, by which I mean an evergreen respect for antique values and an attachment to hierarchical order. In Gaelic Ireland, as in ancient Greece, history appears to have been conceived as akin to poetry. The world of the imagination, the unseen world, has carried for many Irishmen as much conviction as the visible universe. Belief in the supernatural seems to have been a powerful force in ancient Ireland and it would have facilitated acceptance of the new religion. In Christian doctrine, human destiny was envisaged as independent of the earthly environment, which was a temporary abode to be endured rather than adored. Devout Christians were not likely to be attracted to anthropology or geography when Charles Darwin saw geographical distribution as 'the keystone of the laws of creation'. The biblical chronology of Ussher is not now, of course, accepted by the educated, even in its homeland, but it would seem that the spirit in which it was conceived persists, and conditions the view of the human past and the human habitat. One has the impression that, so far as ideas on man's relations with the world of nature are concerned, Darwin might never have voyaged on the Beagle, brooded on Galapagos or patiently reached his view of the universe as a stream of change through time, coming to involve man as a part of nature. There is a deep conviction, in this far western isle, that man has fallen from grace, that the golden age lies in the past, and that national glory can be restored to an imaginary state of purity if men act like the heroes of their legends. For them there is neither evolution nor devolution. The realities both of geography and history are ignored. I like to recall the words of a Welsh colleague, addressed to those of his contemporaries who would dearly like to return to the Middle Ages: 'The odds are that nearly all these hankerers after a past glorious age would find themselves *villeins* in that princely world.'[20]

In the course of the last thirty years or so, Irish academic historians have produced an impressive body of scholarly research, relating particularly to personalities and politics, though social and economic history is creeping in. There has been a conscious effort to get away from traditional attitudes. Wishing to break away from the older emotional brand of Irish history, and convinced that sound general history could not be written without adequate specialist research, scholars have given most of their attention to special periods and problems. There has been an insistence on accuracy, on the critical use of sources and on 'the arid minutiae' of an elaborate bibliographical apparatus. One must admire these scholarly aims so long as they do not come to be regarded as the sole criteria of excellence, so long as curiosity is not stifled by technique and the scaffolding does not obscure the building. It is unfortunate that source-dominated caution has sometimes restricted the vision, and that over-specialisation has made it difficult for the student to look beyond his period or his topic and to see, even if he wished to, the bearing of habitat and heritage on the broad course of history.

The conception of history as a record of great men, events and movements not only has intellectual appeal but it carries prestige, and such history has attractions for the common man – who rarely appears in it – because it gives him a sense of participation in the secrets of power, privilege and patronage and, at the same time, lets him eavesdrop on the scandals and frailties of high society. It is a long way from the geohistory of Bloch and Braudel, which, because it crosses academic frontiers, may come under fire from both sides. It may have distressing bibliographic weaknesses and a lack of discipline, but those who believe in it and try to practise it can endure the criticism if their work brings genuine illumination. I have the impression that Irish historians, in becoming professional, have changed their methods rather than their main interests, and still turn their backs to the land whose history they profess, ignoring habitat and heritage. Geography provides a convenient frame of reference for great events and little else. Of course it might be argued that documentary history is sufficient unto itself, and that geography, archaeology, anthropology and the rest should cultivate their own fields. It is the purpose of these lectures to suggest that all these subjects can be enriched by co-operation. I am encouraged by the remarks of one of the most distinguished of Irish historians, Professor J.C. Beckett, made in his inaugural lecture at this University. They appear to be an afterthought, and bear little relation to the content of his lecture, but to me they carry conviction. He states:[21]

15

The history of Ireland must be based on a study of the relationships between the land and the people. It is in Ireland itself, the physical conditions inspired by life in this country and the effect on those who have lived there, that the historian will find the distinct and continuing character of Irish history.

I read this passage with astonishment and delight. These are views that I have more than once expressed, if with less felicity and authority, since I am not an historian: they made me feel that after all I have been something of an historian all my life.

In the light of this apparent change of emphasis one looks with interest and anticipation at the prospectus of the multi-volume New History of Ireland which is being promoted by a vast scholarly organisation set up under the chairmanship of Professor T.W. Moody and the sponsorship of the Royal Irish Academy, and with Professor Beckett as one of the four editors. Its aim is to provide an authoritative general history of Ireland for the enlightenment of the educated public which will serve also as a background and a stimulus to specialist historical research. It is inspired by the conviction that history means 'the study of human action and thought in the stream of time'. The work is broadly and imaginatively conceived 'in social economic and cultural as well as in political and constitutional terms', will be 'social history in the broad sense' and will take account of 'the changing relations between society and its physical environment'.[22] To this end provision is made for the insertion in the primary narrative of cross-sectional studies of the cultural landscape, and in addition there are to be complementary studies of regional geography, demography, economic life, art and other aspects of Irish culture. All this marks a change in scale and scope from previous general histories of Ireland, and the work will provide an essential frame around which further syntheses can be woven.

The spirit of this great enterprise approaches the French conception of geohistory, but on closer examination the content proposed comes nearer to theohistory, and the stream of time is pre-Darwinian. Despite the remarkable revelations of nearly half a century of archaeological, palaeobotanical and ethnological research, only one of the twenty-two chapters is devoted to the many millennia of human history which witnessed the taming of the land, the establishment of rural settlements, of local attachments to distinctive sub-regions, of enduring modes of life and attitudes; and there seems to be no place for the hidden heritage of the countryside which is the everlasting Ireland. It is from this total heritage, rather than from an isolated élite, that the creative individual emerges. While it is gratifying to see that this is a joint enterprise and that geographers and archaeologists are among the contributors, none is included in the published list of twenty-five scholars making up the advisory board. The scheme departs from the half-enlightened practice of including in conventional history texts a brief geographical introduction which conveniently gets rid of a felt obligation to make some reference to the land whose history is being written,[23] but it is difficult to see how the changing relations between society and its physical environment can properly be fitted into the frame of a conventional narrative history arranged in twenty-two periods, inaugurated in many instances by invaders, rebellions or Acts of Parliament, and emphasising change rather than continuity. 'Social history in the broad sense' should be concerned, one would think, not so much with events as with the links between those events. Nonetheless, one must admire this co-operative enterprise and eagerly await its completion. As a geographer, I must hope that the land of Ireland will emerge as something more than a dead stage for the drama of human history, and that the flowers, in Braudel's words, will reappear every spring.

II

The Irish habitat

If one thinks of habitat as a term of cultural evaluation, deriving its significance from human habit, there seems to be no special justification for giving it priority as an aid to the understanding of regional personality. But it is not only the logic of evolutionary order that makes me place habitat before heritage: when in particular we are dealing with an island, size and shape are critical environmental facts, and the space relations or locational co-ordinates[1] are of paramount importance. These too change their human values with the quickening of communications: for example, an island which had been on the edge of the known world found itself, in the sixteenth century, near the centre of a new world. Yet there is no doubting the simple wisdom of Grenville Cole, a geologist who was also a human geographer: 'to understand the homestead and its home folk, from the thatch of the roof to the colour of the children's hair, we must find the locality on the domed surface of the earth.'[2]

On the globe we look for the smaller of the two larger islands off the north-western coast of Europe, amounting in area to some 30,000 square miles, or about one two-thousandth part of the earth's land surface. Irishmen may well claim that its place in world history is out of proportion to its size, and it is part of my purpose to enquire into the reasons. It belongs to the tattered Atlantic fringe of Europe, the largest of some 5,000 islands and islets lying along the western side of Great Britain in the archipelago which many Irish people refuse to call the British Isles, although there is no simple alternative to this old Celtic title. Both major islands are structurally part of Europe. Their present insularity is recent in terms of human history, coming less than 10,000 years ago, and the seas surrounding them are shallow but fateful floodings of the Continental Shelf. A well-known British geographer, Sir Halford Mackinder, appears to blame the errant waters of the Irish Sea not only for creating Ireland and the Irish problem but for so reducing the width of the larger island in the process as to make it the narrow cradle of two nations (he ignores Wales). In compensation he sees both initiative and a love of liberty resulting from the obstinate diversities of the island peoples.[3]

Insularity is a prime geographical category which we all accept, but if we take the other meaning of the word ('narrow or prejudiced in feelings, ideas or manners') Irishmen would probably apply it, according to their loyalties, only to the people of the other part of the island. Some geographers vainly seeking general laws have claimed that island peoples,

18

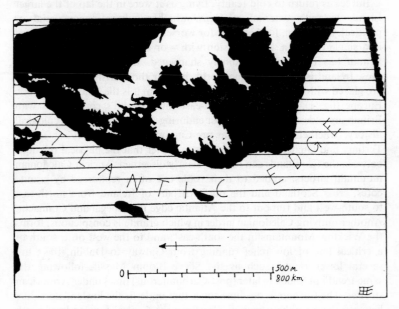

Fig. 1. Two views of Ireland.

because of their insularity, are conservative and culturally homogeneous, but others have discovered that they are precocious and culturally diverse because islands are accessible from all directions. Another generalisation is that islands tend to become overpopulated and to export people – and Ireland provides an outstanding example – but insularity in itself as a natural phenomenon is not a prime cause: time and cultural stage are important factors in their destiny, and behind these are the locational co-ordinates. Who can doubt that Ireland would have had a different heritage and history if it had been located a thousand miles to the west in mid-Atlantic? Alternatively one might speculate on its fate, and on its relations with Great Britain, if it were a much smaller island. If it were to be drowned, Ireland's problems would without doubt be finally solved but it seems that even this solution would only add to England's problems. 'If Ireland were entirely submerged' wrote the archaeologist R.A.S. Macalister, whom I shall have occasion to refer to later for his jaundiced and determinist views on the Irish climate, 'the people of England, subjected to the climate that now afflicts Ireland, would immediately begin to develop all those shortcomings which they are now so ready to find in the Irish.' Worse, because Ireland serves to deflect the beneficent Atlantic drift northwards, were it submerged 'the people of Scotland would be frozen down to the cultural and economic level of the Eskimo'.[4]

But let us return to cold reality. Lying as it were in the lap of the larger island, Ireland's external relations, whether cultural, commercial or political, have been, for better or for worse, overwhelmingly concentrated in a single direction. An obsession with – or revulsion from – links with Britain has been correspondingly sharpened. Looked at with English eyes, Ireland is the end of the world, but for those Irishmen whose eyes are glazed with the glory of Celtic Christiandom it is the centre of Atlantic Europe (fig. 1). It is in the north-east that Ireland's connections with Britain are oldest, closest and most enduring; and if we turn to geological history, whether to the remote pre-Cambrian and Primary or to the Tertiary and Quaternary periods, it is in Ulster that the physical relations between the two islands can be most clearly discerned. Ancient Caledonian mountain girders, eroded to their roots but often reinforced by granite cores, cross Scotland and the northern part of Ireland from north-east to south-west and run out to the Atlantic edge in Donegal and Connacht. Another outlying Caledonian girder in which granite is conspicuous, forms the Wicklow Mountains in the south-east; and to the west of it, south of a critical line of low relief running from Galway to Dublin, there are several lower ranges such as the Slieve Bloom Massif, following the same trend but folded in later (post-Carboniferous) times under Armorican stresses. The Carboniferous limestones that underlie the lowland corridors between these southern massifs also floor the Central Lowlands of north Leinster and east Connacht and stretch northwards into south Ulster.

The lowlands – the term is a relative one, since they rise to several hundred feet in places – terminate in the south of the island against another set of parallel mountain folds trending east and west, the close-packed Armoricans whose eastward extensions run into the Hercynian (Hartz) massifs of Central Europe. Ireland is thus framed on all sides by old fold mountains, and they have mineral lodes containing copper and gold which were among the attractions which it offered in the bronze age to those geologically younger parts of Western Europe where sources of metal were scarce. The land that was to become Ireland, then, may be said to have been held in a pincer grip between the converging western ends of two ancient mountain systems which also embrace Great Britain. Thanks to this convergence it is less elongated and more compact than the larger island (fig. 2) though still having a north–south dichotomy. It is a tectonic unit in its own right, and was already an island, though of somewhat different shape, before Jurassic times. Through successive periods its mountains have been disposed around a central lowland instead of forming a central core as in the popular conception of an island. Moreover, they are much more fragmented than the mountains of Great Britain.

To this fragmentation several factors have contributed. Geomorphology, the study of the evolution of landforms, is a subject of great complexity which I can hardly touch on save in so far as it has a bearing on the nature of the habitat and on economic, cultural and political history. The fragmented topography is part of the island's personality. The geological turbulence of east Ulster has something to do with it, for the Tertiary igneous activity of the Brito-Icelandic province brought with it much faulting and warping, but it is perhaps mainly a matter of climate. The land of Ireland has long been subjected to an oceanic climate, and on the geological time-scale this means more or less continuously since the North Atlantic Ocean was fully opened up perhaps 100 million years ago. Ireland is uniquely wet, not so much in the amount of precipitation it receives as in 'the persistence of the rain and the feebleness of the evaporation'. Professor David Linton considers that this has greatly quickened the erosive processes and has resulted in the characteristic fragmentation of the uplands that distinguishes Ireland from Great Britain.[5] He points out that the further reduction of isolated massifs to many residual hill summits is most marked along the edge of the Atlantic in west Kerry, Connemara, west Mayo and west Donegal. Sea loughs, eroded deep into the land, complete the topographic fragmentation of the far west (fig. 3).

The land that was to become Ireland, moreover, lay near the edge of another ocean in far earlier geological time, for it was never far from the fluctuating margins of that warm mediterranean ocean (Tethys) of which the Mediterranean Sea is a remnant. Successive basins of sedimentation of varying depths gave the ocean margins a variety of marine deposits, and of these none is so characteristic as the limestones which, similarly, give

21

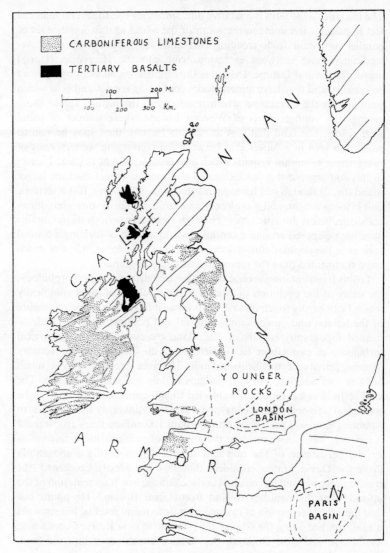

CARBONIFEROUS LIMESTONES

TERTIARY BASALTS

Fig. 2. Caledonian and Armorican convergence.

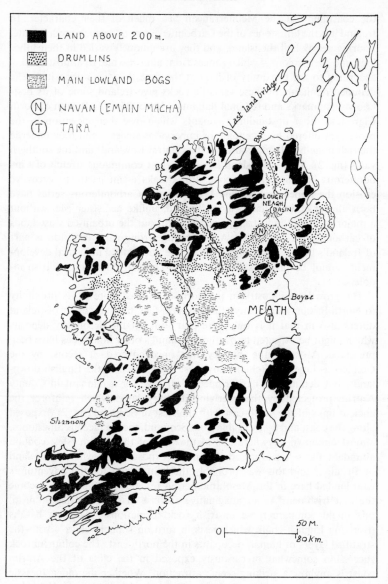

Fig. 3. Fragmented hills, drumlins and lowland bogs.

the coastlands of the Mediterranean Sea much of their character. In Ireland it is the limestones of the Carboniferous period which predominate, flooring nearly half the island, and they are uniquely varied in their lithology and their colour – which ranges from almost white to almost black – according to the proximity of land at the time they were deposited. The denuded remnants of these versatile rocks give Ireland some of its best-known landmarks and regional habitats – Benbulbin, the Burren of north Clare and other upstanding remnants which owe their elevation to the protection offered by a capping of impervious shales – and they underlie the rich bone-building pastures of the Central Lowlands and the southern vales (fig. 2). This little island has the largest continuous stretch of Carboniferous limestones in Europe. But thanks again partly to excessive erosion the upper coal-bearing layers of the Carboniferous series have been almost entirely lost, leaving Ireland, unlike her sister isle, without a major source of industrial power and without the urbanised wastelands of carboniferous capitalism. A continuing strong rural tradition is part of Ireland's heritage: the blame for its late and limited industrial development cannot be placed solely on British colonial policy or on Irish indolence.

The growth of industry in the north-east owes more to its proximity to North Britain than to any other physical fact, but this corner of Ireland differs also in that it is only here that some of the Secondary deposits which might be expected to overlie the island's older limestones have been preserved. Most of the country was once covered, it seems, by the Cretaceous limestone (chalk) now best represented in the English downlands, but denudation has stripped it off save for a remnant in County Antrim protected by the overlying Tertiary lavas which reinforce the ancient links of the north-east with the west of Scotland (fig. 2). Exposed along the coast and easily visible from Scotland, the Cretaceous limestones, almost unknown anywhere else in the west of the British Isles, contain abundant flints 'unsurpassed in surface exposures elsewhere in Ireland or Britain',[6] and this was probably their attraction for the adventurers who landed here in the Mesolithic period (c. 8000–4000 B.C.) to become the first Irishmen. As an imaginative exercise in symbolic determinism, one might compare these un-Irish rock formations – Scottish basalts overlying English chalk which rests in turn on slippery clays – with the stratified layers of human occupants in the north-east. The colourful rock succession somewhat precariously exposed in the cliffs of the Antrim coast is anyhow a striking scenic attraction. Whether the older Jurassic limestones were ever deposited over any part of Ireland is doubtful, but it is certain that the absence of their oolitic freestones has been an architectural and artistic deprivation for which an abundance of hard limestones and tough granites has hardly compensated. Moreover, the Central Lowlands might have become a cradle for the Irish nation if they had

PLATE 1

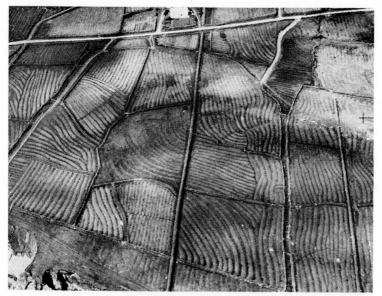

a Abandoned spade ridges of former infield, now striped. Glen, Clare Island, County Mayo. (Photograph: J. K. St Joseph, Cambridge University Collection: copyright reserved.)

b Prehistoric cultivation ridges (width about 4½ feet) revealed by turf-cutters in the townland of Carrownaglogh, Co. Mayo. (Photograph: R. Glasscock.)

PLATE 2

Decorated stone basin in right-hand recess of the eastern chamber in the great burial mound at Knowth, County Meath. The passage leading to the chamber is 35m in length. (Photograph: Commissioners of Public Works in Ireland.)

been endowed with the kindlier Secondary and Tertiary deposits such as, in the basins of London and Paris, have provided a rich nuclear area and facilitated, since early medieval times, the concentration of metropolitan wealth and political power. The Shannon estuary, an entry of great promise more than once in the past, might then have become the gateway to an Irish heartland, but it is doubtful whether under the most favourable conditions it could have competed with the eastern entries. As it is, the Central Lowlands, which over wide distances average some 250 feet in height, are tilted down towards the west, and the Shannon drains or fails to drain about half the lowland area. A powerful central Irish kingdom did not emerge at any time (fig. 3). Uisneach in Westmeath 'the navel of Gaelic Ireland', was central only in a theoretical, geometrical sense, and Athlone, in the same county, became a major centre of communication for the island only when Radio Eireann was given the freedom of the air. For not only do the lowlands lack the centripetal pull of a youthful basin of sedimentation, but their levelled surfaces are littered as we shall see with assorted glacial deposits which have clogged the drainage, given rise to bogs, and made movement difficult save where gravel ridges have provided dry routeways (fig. 3).

No other European country has such a fragmented peripheral arrangement of mountain land, and if this has given her a diversified scenic heritage which is an abiding asset, it has also brought many social, economic and political problems. In this respect the broken German lands of Central Europe, where political unification was late and incomplete, offer the closest parallel. If Ireland, as pious politicians proclaim, is a God-given island, then the maxim 'divide and rule' must be attributed to higher authority than Dublin Castle. For would-be conquerors, an illogical distribution of stubborn massifs brought many difficulties. For reasons which may be linked with their distance from the more powerful erosive forces of the oceanic coast some of the most extensive areas of high land occur on the invaders' coast: indeed the largest exposure of mountain granites in the British Isles overlooks Dublin, and the greatest expanse of basic igneous rocks frowns above Belfast; and both have been embarrassments as well as adornments to the capital cities. It is a remarkable tribute to the strength of native traditions that archaic solid wheeled carts and other ethnological survivals could be found within sight of both cities until late in last century. For reasons we shall look into, the hill margins were the favoured habitats of the first farmers who had penetrated into most parts of the island by the beginning of the second millennium B.C. In time the hills came to serve as territorial bases for local clans and patriotisms; and the multiplicity of small rival kingdoms in Gaelic Ireland, which tempted in the invader and delayed unification, was facilitated by topographic fragmentation. Later the hills became regions of refuge. The Gaelic language finds its last precarious footholds in the hilly peninsulas of the far west, and because the Gaeltacht was thus reduced to many separate scattered 'islands' – which are further fragmented so that there are in fact over thirty 'islets' – the chances of the survival of Gaelic, still less of its revival, are greatly reduced as compared, for example, with Welsh, which clings tenaciously to the solid mountain core of the country stretching almost unbroken from Caernarvon to Glamorgan. I am not saying that this environmental factor alone explains the contrast but that, in trying to understand such cultural distributions, habitat as well as heritage and history should be taken into account.

The only wide breach in the mountain rim of Ireland is the fifty-mile stretch of coast between Dublin and Dundalk, and here successive in-comers through the centuries – passage grave builders, Celtic kings, Viking raiders and traders, Cistercian monks, Anglo-Norman barons and English kings – established their main base. Like the other 'nuclear areas' of west European countries, it has the advantage of good well-drained soils and a relatively low rainfall, providing an assured base of agricultural wealth. This is the only part of Ireland where the annual rainfall drops below thirty inches, and Meath is the only coastal county whose hills fail to reach 1000 feet (fig. 3). By contrast, in the far south-west are the dripping mountain peninsulas of Kerry, a refuge area (for the red deer for instance) where, in the words of Grenville Cole, 'the essential difficulties of Ireland are emphasized and concentrated'. Here, around the summits the precipita-tion exceeds 100 inches, and if one were to seek a critical limit to profitable arable husbandry in Ireland, it might be found in the fifty-inch annual rainfall line. It is within this line that the most extensive areas of blanket bog occur.

Yet it is not the south-west but the peninsula in the north-east that has repeatedly and most conspicuously demonstrated its separate identity among the regions of Ireland, and we must ask if there are contributing geographical factors apart from its proximity to Scotland. There are, as we have seen, certain geological differences, but even the most extreme environmentalist would not claim that Ulster's fiery independence is related to its monopoly of Eocene volcanism! It is only towards the rather bleak north coast of the island that the Carboniferous limestones of the Central Lowlands fail to extend a friendly arm. The climate is cooler here the whole year round and the growing season shorter. The landscape in places approaches the austere. Tree-fruits such as chestnuts and walnuts rarely ripen and one will see no sweet-scented cowslips in the fields. As a habitat it is more familiar and attractive to Scotsmen than to lowland Englishmen. Topographically, Ulster displays the characteristic frag-mentation even better than the other three provinces: indeed, when one looks at the full record of habitat, heritage and history, one begins to think of Ulster as the most Irish of all the regions and to see the essential

Fig. 4. A drumlin cluster in County Down. (Sketch by David Evans.)

difficulties of Ireland emphasised and concentrated not in the south-west but in the northern province.

The north-east has its own central lowlands in the Lough Neagh basin, which is richly endowed with varied glacial deposits and which might have provided a regional nuclear area if its heart were not drowned under the extensive waters of its eponymous lake, which with the outflowing river Bann has been an historic divide (fig. 3). Most of the drainage of Ulster fans out northwards from a devious watershed which never lies far from the historic frontier of Ulster. This border zone is the drumlin belt, consisting of the scrapings of the Ulster hills deposited under the ice as it moved into the Central Lowlands. The shapely streamlined mounds of boulder clay, in their tens of thousands, appear on a map of surface morphology as a necklace of beads some thirty miles wide suspended between Donegal Bay and Strangford Lough (fig. 3). The vast majority of Irish place-names having *druim* or drum (a hill) as prefix or suffix occurs in this area.[7] It is not a continuous belt, for the higher hills stand out like islands from the sea of drumlins, but at elevations up to about 600 feet the typical border landscape is a confusion of little hills and of winding streams, small lakes, and bogs, testifying to the difficulty with which water finds a way out (fig. 4). In protohistoric times, before the tangled woods were cleared, lakelets drained, and little bogs reclaimed, all this belt provided a defence in depth for the kingdom of Ulster whose

27

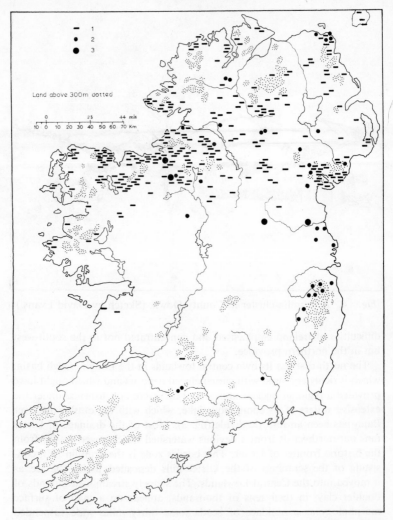

Fig. 5. Distribution of early forms of megalithic tombs, Middle to Late Neolithic. 1. Court graves in long cairns. 2. Passage graves in round cairns. 3. Passage grave cemeteries.

frontier against the south, the legendary Black Pig's Dyke – in reality a series of protective earthworks guarding the few ways through – was built in a forward position within the drumlin belt. In middle Neolithic times, approximately through the third millennium, that characteristic northern monument, the megalithic court grave set in its long cairn, penetrates into the higher parts of the drumlin belt but does not extend south of it into the Central Lowlands (fig. 5). In terms of megalithic religion, Ulster and north Connacht stand out as a culture area having its closest overseas links with the Clyde region and the Isle of Man, though the Boyne culture with its decorated passage graves set in round cairns is also represented here and there in the north as a minority faith. At many periods the southern margins of the drumlin belt appear to have been a cultural divide: for example, this is the transition zone between northern and southern dialects both in Gaelic and Anglo-Irish.

I have the impression that social psychologists in their studies of environmental perception tend to reduce the physical environment to a uniform matrix and take insufficient account of its many varieties. At the risk of being called hopelessly old-fashioned, I turn to that masterly observer of nature, W.H. Hudson. He writes:[8]

It is probable that we who are country born and bred are affected in more ways and more profoundly than we know by our surroundings. The nature of the soil we live on, the absence or presence of running water, of hills, rocks, woods, open spaces; every feature of the landscape, the vegetative and animal life – everything in fact that we see, hear, smell and feel – enters not into the body only, but the soul, and helps to shape and colour it. Equally important in its action on us are the conditions created by man himself – situation, size, form and the arrangements of the houses in the village; its traditions, customs and social life.

I have heard another well-known naturalist, Dr Fraser Darling, speak in similar vein from his observations in the Scottish Highlands and Islands, commenting on the vision and imagination of crofters living on naked mountainsides and on the egalitarian attitudes prevailing in a community which is always under observation. And in a recent perceptive book of Irish reminiscences Nora Robertson speculates on 'how much the open views, the stony furzy fields and the far-off hills have affected the dwellers of the Celtic fringe'.[9]

It is in this spirit that I would ask you to look at the drumlin country. The landscape has a charming intimacy. Roads winding their way through bushy hollows among the little hills bring constantly changing views, but horizons are always near and the vision restricted (fig. 4). One might think of the moulded drumlins as moulding, in turn, the outlook of the farmers who dwell among them. Much of the drumlin country is Orange country. For reasons known to history, the most fertile parts of Ulster were occupied by Protestant planters in the seventeenth century. The deep drumlin soils, previously utilised mainly for grazing, responded to the labour of a Protestant people who saw virtue in hard work. Many small patches of flax were grown, and large families kept busy with its preparation, spinning, weaving, finishing and marketing. The topography favoured small territorial units: both the townlands and the farm holdings

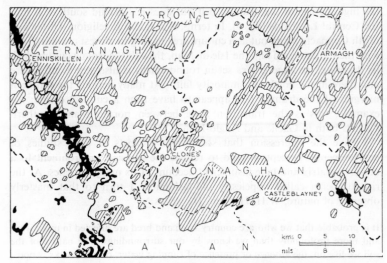

Fig. 6. Religious confusion on the Ulster border. Distribution of Protestants and Roman Catholics in the drumlin belt in South Ulster, 1911, by townlands. Townlands with a Protestant majority are ruled: those with a Catholic majority are blank. (Reproduced from Crown copyright records in the Public Record Office, London, by permission of the Controller of H.M.S.O.)

are smaller than the Irish average. One thinks of the west of Ireland as the most congested part of the country in the nineteenth century, but in 1841, when the amount of arable land per head of the rural population in County Galway was three-and-a-half acres, it was only one-and-a-quarter acres in County Armagh. Competition for land was keen, and it was among the episcopalian drumlins[10] in north Armagh that the Orange Order had its rural roots in 1795. When you see the big drumlins, whether at Rossnowlagh on Donegal Bay or at Killyleagh on Strangford Lough, you may expect to hear the noise of the big drums in the month of July. But the rocky hills which interrupt the drumlins have retained a Roman Catholic population, and this also applies to the badly-drained lowlands of south Fermanagh and central Cavan where the soils are exceptionally sticky. Here a map showing religious distributions is a mosaic of Protestant islands in a Catholic sea (fig. 6). It is through this confusion that the political border between Northern Ireland and the Republic takes a tortuous course that was preordained by the old county boundaries. The border belt became a smuggler's paradise, and sometimes a battleground, regarded by both sides as the last frontier of the British

Empire. The interactions of physical, historic, religious and economic factors have kept alive the suspicions of an ancient frontier. A County Monaghan writer, Patrick Kavanagh, has given us a memorable picture of one of the poorer parts of the drumlin country, of the little hills with their sunny sides and their black sides, of 'the little fields and scraping poverty, where each person was keeping up spite to at least two of his neighbours'.[11] No doubt the reasons are complex, but the Republican border counties of Monaghan, Cavan, Leitrim and Donegal are among the poorest in the whole country, having the lowest net incomes and the highest rates of unemployment and emigration.[12]

To the south of the drumlin belt in the Central Lowlands, where the ice melted unevenly in its slow retreat, surface features resulting from glaciation take a different form. It is true that there are clusters of fat drumlins towards the hilly western margins, penetrating to the coast and into the sea in Clew Bay. They are not particularly Protestant, and they serve as a reminder, if such were needed, that landforms of themselves, without heritage and history, hold no compelling power. The typical deposits in the Central Lowlands are composed of sands and gravels, taking a variety of forms: successive curving end-moraines; broad stretches of hummocky kame-moraine; levelled outwash materials such as occur in the Curragh of Kildare – as attractive to prehistoric settlers as they have been to horses and armies in our own times – or again worm-like ridges (eskers) left behind by subglacial streams. Lying between these various deposits are many lakes, level stretches of alluvium or extensive peat bogs (the so-called basin or red bogs) providing obstacles to communications which could be easily by-passed only where linear moraines or eskers provided a dry footing for routeways. The favoured coastal strip between Dublin and Dundalk, rising to more than 400 feet in the Hill of Tara, is almost free of bogs and other encumbrances and is well drained by the Boyne and the Liffey, which reach the sea through picturesque incised valleys (fig. 3). To the north of the drumlin belt the Ulster basin too became a glacial dumping ground. In fact the most extensive series of kame-moraines in Ireland occupies the heart of Ulster, to the west of Lough Neagh in County Tyrone. They extend into the hills, where many of the moraines are now blanketed with peat, but being more continuous, higher-lying and better drained than those of central Ireland they were a well-peopled habitat in the Neolithic period.

Such, in bald outline, was the physical inheritance of this Atlantic island. We must now clothe the naked land with the forests which, after 10,000 years, have almost entirely disappeared, leaving hardly a trace on the landscape. The reconstructed history of their gradual reduction by the hand of man and the teeth of his grazing animals provides many clues to the changing cultural and economic life of the Irish people and to the manifold interrelations between forest history and folk tradition. Before the last remnants of ice had melted from the mountain cwms, a forest vegetation creeping back across north-western Europe had joined the sparse Alpine flora and driven it into the high hills, though some species have retained a foothold on the exposed west coast even down to sea-level. When men first reached Ireland, on present evidence not long before 6000 B.C., they found a land forested almost everywhere save where it was broken by lakes and swamps. They came into the north-east across the North Channel, at its narrowest only thirteen miles wide and then considerably narrower, and if these pioneers of Upper Palaeolithic ancestry whose descendants have the best claim to be called Irishmen seem remote to those accustomed to the time-scale of recorded history, it should be remembered that, in 6000 B.C., urban settlements in the Near East such as Jericho were already well-established. It is a measure of its remoteness from the centres of urban civilisation that urbanisation hardly touched most of Ulster until the seventeenth century A.D.

This remoteness too delayed and restricted the returning vegetation, though a few species of the evergreen Lusitanian flora were able to spread into the western peninsulas from an area of interglacial survival in the south-west. Most plants and animals had to cross the Irish Sea, and this they were able to do by temporary bridges provided by morainic ridges which were not submerged until the last melt of Scandinavian ice had restored a lowered glacial sea-level to its approximate pre-glacial position. Many plants that were common in pre-glacial times, for example the rhododendron, maple, hornbeam, spruce and silver fir, did not return and were re-introduced by man in recent times. The last land bridge to be severed ran from Inishowen to Islay, Jura and the western Grampians (fig. 3), and latecomers had to depend on this hyperborean umbilical cord whose track was later followed by saints and sinners alike moving to and fro across the turbulent seas between western Scotland and the north of Ireland. We know that many species of plants and some smaller animals, among them snakes, moles, weasels, and toads, did not make it. Thus Ireland's flora and fauna were severely restricted, the number of native species, for example (about 1000), being less than two-thirds the figure for Great Britain, whose land bridge with the continent survived longer. Many of the most conspicuous plants that flourish around the Irish coasts are not native species: their variety is a tribute to the mild climate and to human enterprise. Many landscapes that are regarded as typically Irish are in fact the mirror of man.

Beech and lime, sycamore, sweet-chestnut and horse-chestnut and nearly all the conifers are not native trees, and even such a colourful contributor to the coastlands as the ubiquitous fuchsia, a native of Chile, may not have been here a hundred years. And the truly native shrubs and bushes whose blooms brighten the hillsides and the hedges – gorse and broom, hawthorn and blackthorn – as well as the wild flowers of open country, found light and room to spread their bounty only as man began to clear the high forest. Palaeobotanists tell us of the species of which the woods were composed and the order of their coming as the climate ameliorated after the ice age: willow and birch, hazel, pine, alder, oak, elm and ash. As the forest spread over the land, some of the larger animals took refuge in the limited open spaces. The giant deer with its great spread of antlers was severely handicapped and may have been finally exterminated by man. In the early post-glacial period it had multiplied so freely, apparently in the absence of human predators, that it takes its popular name, the Irish Elk, from its best-known European habitat. But potential domesticates among the native fauna were as rare as potential cultigens among the plants. All the most important domesticated plants and animals had to be imported before man could begin to produce food, and with two principal exceptions, the potato and the ass, which are popularly regarded as the most Irish of all, they were brought to Ireland long before recorded history.

But what shall we say about the Irish climate, or having broached the topic, how shall we stop? It would seem that, whereas the living landscape has been profoundly altered in human times, climate has remained much the same ever since the great fluctuations of the glacial period and the minor ups and downs of late glacial readjustments were succeeded by a familiar Atlantic climate as warm ocean waters flooded back seven or eight thousand years ago and restored the island to its approximate pre-glacial shape not long before 3000 B.C. Much has been made, it is true, of palaeobotanical evidence of vegetational changes which seems to indicate a worsening of climate during the late Bronze Age, from about 600 B.C., in what is termed the sub-Atlantic period. Historical evidence, too, points to a phase of wet and stormy climate in the Middle Ages, after about A.D. 1250. The significance of these wet periods in Ireland has probably been exaggerated. Some climatologists hold that such fluctuations as have occurred do not lie seriously outside the possibilities of the present-day climate. They point out that instability is a characteristic of the oceanic climate of Western Europe, which depends not so much on the regularity of the sun's apparent movement as on the vagaries of oceanic and general atmospheric circulation. There is evidence which suggests, however, that the climates of the Atlantic and sub-Boreal periods (c. 5000–600 B.C.) were warmer than those of protohistoric and historic times by an estimated two degrees (C). In Denmark, Iversen and Troels-Smith have supported the theory of a post-glacial climatic optimum by studying variations in the pollens of three evergreen Atlantic plants, ivy mistletoe and holly. In this view, our present climate was established in sub-Atlantic times.

A changing vegetational balance, however, may be explained in terms of human interference and does not necessarily imply climatic change.

And even if it can be proved that there were phases of climatic deterioration, one is suspicious of attempts to link them directly with periods of declining prosperity and cultural stagnation. While a succession of cool wet summers would have been serious for corn growers depending on bread, it would have had less effect on a pastoral people living largely on 'whitemeats' (milk products), for 'the more rain, the more grass for the bull'. Professor R.A.S. Macalister, to whose deterministic views I have already referred, has said that 'the history of Ireland is a vain beating against the iron bars of its physical limitations', and has claimed that 'an adverse fluctuation of climate in Ireland *must* produce physical moral and material atrophy'. He has charted his own estimate of the rise and fall of Irish civilisation against the graph of the supposed ups and downs of climate, and he finds the agreement highly satisfactory. It was climate, he held, that had 'set bounds to the march of the Irish nation'.[13] But to judge from the energy and eloquence with which Macalister in his later days, following his early 'Gaelic enthusiasm', attacked the Irish achievement, the Irish climate had set no bounds to his own vigour. It is perhaps not surprising that Professor D.A. Binchy could write of 'the imaginative and often conflicting speculations of archaeologists and devotees of that curious science that calls itself prehistory'.[14] Yet the special circumstances of early Celtic Ireland, with its long protohistoric twilight, cry out for better understanding and co-operation between linguists, archaeologists and historians, not to mention geographers.

It is in connection with environmental deterioration that the problem of climatic change becomes critical, for it has generally been held responsible for the extraordinary development of peat, or turf: it keeps its older name in Ireland, except in the north-east. No less than one-sixth of the land is or has been covered with peat, and in recent centuries, with the almost total destruction of the remaining woodlands, the landscape and economy of large parts of the country, especially in the west, have been dominated by bogland. The sight and scent of turf are evocative of traditional rural life, and like the peasant mind, the peat bogs hold the past in their depths. Thanks to their preservative powers, they contain a record of vegetational and human history to supplement the meagre written record. Man down the ages has been a tool-loser as well as a tool-user, and artefacts of many kinds, lost in the bogs (or deliberately buried in the hope of recovery or as a ritual act) when discovered by turf-cutters or by archaeologists, can be placed in chronological order according to their stratigraphical position and equated with environmental changes through several thousand years. For the peat also preserves millions of grains of pollen which enable the palaeobotanist to reconstruct the vegetation succession not only of the bogs themselves but also of the adjacent landscapes which contributed their wind-blown pollens. In many bogs the evidence of forest history is more direct, for two or three layers of tree remains may be found, testifying to periods of forest regeneration. Similarly, wooden artefacts (or articles of clothing) which are otherwise both perishable and undocumented provide valuable evidence for the historian and the archaeologist. However we may explain the origins and the prevalence of the bogs, what is certain is that many of them have been formed in human times and that they are an intimate part of the personality of the island.

We know that, in historic times, the Irish bogs served as places of refuge, providing even in many parts of the lowlands hiding places as secure as the mountain massifs: together, mountains and bogs made the subjugation of the whole country well nigh impossible. Anglo-Norman settlement was most successful in the almost bog-free lowlands of the east and south which have been predominantly English in speech, at any rate in the towns, since the Middle Ages. A distinction must be made, topographically, morphologically and genetically, between the lowland red bogs or basin bogs, which are also confusingly termed 'raised bogs', and the well-named blanket bogs (also called climatic bogs), which are typical of the uplands but which clothe the land in places right down to the western seas, covering areas which were originally for the most part forested. The former occupy inter-drumlin hollows, ill-drained basins and lake and river margins, especially in the central and western parts of the lowlands; and beginning as fenlands they may have accumulated peat to a depth of twenty or even forty feet. The blanket bogs occur in areas of high precipitation and high humidity, but they are rarely more than from six to eight feet deep and it has been assumed that most of them originated in the sub-Atlantic climatic deterioration of the last millennium B.C. by the smothering of the forest cover. The lowest layers of some blanket bogs, however, have been dated to sub-Boreal times, between 2500 and 600 B.C., when the climate is thought to have been drier and more continental than at present, and indeed the reality of the sub-Atlantic deterioration in Ireland has been questioned. The pollen evidence points to many small fluctuations in prehistoric as in historic times rather than to a few periods of dramatic and catastrophic worsening of climate.

The question is raised, therefore, whether man himself, whose association with the bogs has been close, in one way or another, since prehistoric times, was responsible for the initiation of blanket bogs in the hills, for example by clearing patches of forest for agriculture and exhausting the soil. Even in late Boreal times, before agriculture had been introduced, evidence is accumulating to show that man was capable of bringing about vegetational change. In the north-east, in areas adjacent to the fishing grounds of Lough Neagh and the Bann, patches of forests were cleared by fire, and hazel scrub, perhaps encouraged as a source of food, came to occupy the clearings. From the middle of the fourth millennium, such vegetational changes can be correlated with the clear archaeological evidence of agricultural activities, following the example of pioneer researches in Denmark which established the antiquity of what they term *landnam* (land taking). In the fossil soil below the blanket peat, for example in several places among the kame-moraines in County Tyrone, one finds evidence of the burning of trees in the form of charcoal, and abundant human artefacts as well as the foundations of habitations dateable to the second half of the fourth millennium. The pollen records from adjacent peats show a sharp decline of tree pollens, particularly of the elm (which seems to have been used as an indicator of suitable well-drained farming soils and probably also as a source of fodder for cattle and sheep or goats) and an increase of the pollens of herbs and grasses, including that of introduced cereals, wheat and barley. There follows an increase of birch and hazel pollens as forest weeds take over the abandoned clearings. Grass and herbs, including the tell-tale ribwort plantain, increase again with grazing activity.[15] One may sum up the general evidence obtained in this way from many parts of the country by saying that it gives us a picture of successive phases of forest clearance by axe and fire, and of partial re-generation, with varying emphasis from time to time and from place to place on arable and pastoral farming. This approach to farming history can be applied down to quite recent times and used to supplement, and perhaps to correct, the documentary evidence. Long before written history begins, Professor G.F. Mitchell writes, 'the countryside was a mosaic, areas of virgin forest alternating with tillage patches, rough pastures and secondary forest in various stages of regeneration'.[16] By the time recorded history begins probably few forested areas were untouched by man, and when one realises the complexities of ecological change through millennia one could wish that historians had displayed as much interest in the supposed virginity of the Irish woodlands in Elizabeth's time as they have in that of the lady herself.[17] It is in the light of this long fight of farmers and herders against the forest that one should see the Irish countryman's continuing hostility to trees, and the sad fact that, before modern re-afforestation schemes, wooded areas occupied little more than one per cent of the surface of the land. Even today the figure is less than two-and-a-half per cent. There may be a kernel of truth in an Irish rhyme which runs:

> Ireland was thrice beneath the ploughshare,
> Thrice it was wooded, and thrice was bare.

But the problem of the origin, or origins, of Ireland's vast expanses of blanket peat is far from being solved. It stretches the imagination to believe that man was responsible for all the wastelands of the west. Where climatic conditions are extreme, a few sunless summers may have been enough to cause soil saturation and the death of forests. And it must be admitted that some of the sub-peat soils on sites known to have been cultivated in prehistoric times show little sign of the heavy leaching, leading to the formation of iron pan, which would provide a rational explanation for waterlogging gleying and the initiation of peat. But, however changes in soil and vegetation began, they were accelerated in various ways by human activity. In these Atlantic environments, it has been said, 'where men first worked, peats have most formed'.[18]

All in all, one wonders why, in the beginning, men chose to live in this far-off rain-soaked land. Would they have stayed if on reaching these shores from sunnier parts, they could have heard a long-range forecast: 'it will be wet almost everywhere, but a few sunny intervals may occur from time to time', or if, on some May morning whose brilliance may have tempted them to land on a shore bright with May blossom against the dark forest, they had heard – and I quote a recent forecast for a day in late May – 'the temperatures will soar into the high fifties (F)'? Certainly there were game and fish in plenty, and abundant supplies of flint and other hard stones for tool-making. Were they prospectors, refugees, or shipwrecked voyagers? Was it human curiosity that brought them here, an urge to follow the setting sun, or perhaps a family quarrel? – a motive irrational enough to appeal to an historian such as Gibbon. But having come, for whatever reason, they stayed and multiplied.

I am aware that some Irishmen consider their climate to be the best in the world. Tacitus found the British climate objectionable and a modern Italian has described it as the worst in the civilised world but it too, for one of its most celebrated champions, Charles II, was the best in the world. Men will see virtue in the particular climate in which their own genius has flowered. Climate contributes to the personality of Ireland and its people in very many ways, and neither would be the same were it drier, sunnier and more extreme in temperature range. To be sure, there are compensations. This green isle has been called Europe's decompression chamber. The constantly changing skies and lights are an endless source of delight. To quote the closing lines of an epitaph on an Irish lady which might be applied to Ireland herself: 'She also painted in water colours. For of such is the Kingdom of Heaven.' I will not weary you with climatic statistics, which are readily available in text-books. There has been much speculation on the possible relationship between the warm humid conditions of south-western Ireland and the soft accents and supposed laziness of the Kerryman. Professor Walter Fitzgerald, in a pioneer work on Irish historical geography, expressed the guardedly deterministic view that the increase in winter cold as one travels from the south-west to the north-east 'explains such physical alertness as the northerners claim to possess'.[19] In general, it may be said that constantly changing weather brings a sense of uncertainty and perhaps encourages an indifference to time and a predilection for gambling and for alcohol.[20] The heavy precipitation and the clouds and mists which allow the sun to be seen, on average, only one day in three, nourish an abundant growth of grass, and the mild temperatures keep it green throughout the year. Human habitations, so long as they can be kept dry, can be simple structures needing no elaborate defences against extreme cold. Wind is a more significant factor, and a more important drying agent, than the sun: unless summers were appreciably warmer in Neolithic times it is difficult to see how wheat could have been successfully harvested if the forest clearings were not large enough to admit the wind. If there was indeed a 'thermal maximum' at the time of maximum marine transgression a century or two before 3000 B.C., could this be one of the golden ages enshrined in the long memory of the Irish?

The dominant tradition of the Irish countryside has long been a pastoral one. Today, about half the improved land is in pasture and in addition there is abundant rough grazing almost everywhere in mountain or bog. For long stretches of Irish history the cattleman has been king. Rival claims to the best pastures have been a potent source of friction, and the violence of the stockman, which has been so much in evidence similarly in Spanish history, has left a troublesome heritage of endemic lawlessness. Under the climatic conditions prevailing in Ireland a grass cover protects the soil from excessive leaching, and when it luxuriates on good soils, as in County Meath, some stock farmers regard it as a sin to break the sod. But where soils are heavy, permanent pastures tend to become poached, waterlogged and rushy unless they are broken up from time to time; and it is established practice in areas of mixed farming 'to take the plough around the farm', a practice that seems to have evolved from the traditional method of 'outfield' cultivation. The soil is an environmental element which, for some geographers, provides the best single clue to historic regional character because its nature is a summation of many other environmental factors such as solid and surface geology, topography, hydrology and climate. It has an intimate bearing on the methods of land-use adopted and through them on the organisation of rural society.

Thanks to the island's diversities, a soil map of Ireland is a mosaic of some thirty soil-types, but many of them, occupying in aggregate about a third of the surface area, are fit only to support rough grazing. Another third of the country has soils with a limited use-range, leaving another third with soils that can be classed as having a wide use-range, but these are characteristically fragmented and located in different parts of the lowlands.[21] The most widespread of the better soils are classed as grey-brown Podzolics, owing their colour and relative acidity to the washing down of minerals by leaching. To appreciate their nature one may contrast them with the thin red soils of sunnier climates such as those of Southern

Europe which lack a good supply of humus and are coloured by minerals brought to the surface by strong evaporation. They are too dry to support permanent grass but, to tap such fertility as they have, the farmer need exploit only the surface layer for his annual crops, and tools of cultivation are traditionally simple, including hoes of various kinds and the light wooden plough (*araire*). This is an oversimplification but it will serve to suggest relationships between climate, soil, land-use and social life which historians have tended to ignore. Similarly, it has been said of hoe-cultivators in parts of tropical Africa that they have only to tickle the soil and it laughs with a harvest, though it should be added that, if the soil is over-exposed, its chemistry can be disastrously affected. Under the climatic conditions prevailing in the fertile lowlands of Western Europe, the downwash of plant nutrients is roughly balanced by evaporation and the fertility extends to some depth in the soil to give the rich loams or brown earths. Among the technological improvements which helped Western Europe to emerge into the light of civilisation in the early Celtic period was the iron-shod plough with a heavy sod-cutting coulter, capable of deeper penetration, and when later the mould-board was added to invert the furrow-slice, the fertility of the soil was exploited more efficiently, and increased agricultural production geared to the institutional framework of feudalism helped to speed society into the Middle Ages.

Under the conditions prevailing in Ireland, different methods of land-use were evolved, adjusted to a predominantly pastoral economy and in the first place, before the coming of iron tools, to fairly light well-drained soils which were frequently obstructed with stones. A heavy plough was introduced at some stage during the early Celtic period – it is archaeologically attested and is described in some detail in the Old Irish law tracts – but its effective use was probably restricted to the more favourable soils which were neither too light nor too heavy. Anglo-Norman agriculture, utilising openfields of some kind, seems to have been most successful on such soils, where a heavy plough could be used to advantage. In the refuge areas where the old population was able to survive in strength, a wheel-less wooden plough of *araire* type was used into the last century, and on analogy with other parts of north-western Europe it was a prehistoric introduction. At this point, it is important to bear in mind the distinction between infield and outfield, a topic to which I will return later. The infield was a carefully selected patch of relatively dry soil adjacent to the settlement and indeed determining its site, and to judge from examples which survived into recent times it was maintained in more or less permanent cultivation by the use of manure supplied by wintering livestock – often hoarded in the dwelling houses. The infield plots were small, and under these conditions a short wooden plough which was sometimes drawn by the horse's tail was adequate.[22] But outfield cultivation, that is the periodic exploitation of heavily grazed land usually located uphill from the settlement, was another matter. The sward, compacted by the treading of animals, tended to become a tough mat composed of the fibrous roots of perennial grasses, sedges and rushes, plants which are rich in decay-resistant fats and waxes. I have heard farmers say that old grassland on the sticky-soiled drumlins of Fermanagh is 'too tough for the plough'. The spade-turned cultivation ridge – the so-called lazy-bed – which as we shall see appears to be of great antiquity, proved to be the best method of coping with these conditions.

There is no more diagnostic feature of the cultural landscape of Ireland than abandoned bundles of cultivation ridges (pl. 1a). They are so much a part of the rural scene in many areas that I make no excuse for introducing them as an element of the habitat. I would see them as an index of the continuity and character of Irish rural culture. The spade-ridge is still the preferred mode of cultivating garden crops in many parts of the country, and it is claimed that this method increases the yield. In the west, and in some hilly districts elsewhere, it is still the common method of growing field crops, especially potatoes; and corn was similarly planted in raised beds until recent times. Traces of them are visible over a far wider area, particularly on the hillsides, where those abandoned in famine times may stand out boldly while older examples are visible only when a low sun or a sprinkling of ground frost or snow throws them into relief. It could be said that the face of old Ireland is wrinkled with their tracks. Most of them were fashioned by spade and shovel, but some were roughed out with the plough, and others were made with the mattock (in the south-west) or by the mis-named breast plough (in the north). The spade ridges were not dug over – hence the name lazy-bed – but sods from the strips between them were inverted on to the beds, which were further raised by shovelling on soil from the trenches. The advantages of the 'lazy-bed' in an Atlantic environment may readily be shown. Not only is the seed-bed raised above the water table, but the trench serves both as a drainage channel and as a source of mineral soil, and it goes deep enough to break through any iron-pan that may have been deposited by heavy leaching. The ridges allow the soil to be warmed from the sides as well as the top and they were, moreover, sometimes sloped to catch the maximum sun. They have further the considerable advantage of burying and reducing weeds. The narrow Irish spade, in its many varieties, is not primarily a digging tool but is designed to undercut the sod and invert it, in fact to do the work of an efficient plough. In thinking of the origins and prevalence of what might be termed a ridge-culture-complex, two facts should be borne in mind. One is the fibrous nature of the grass-mat which tends to develop on undisturbed grazing land on acid soils, making it easier, with primitive tools, to undercut the sod, horizontally, than to drag a plough or to dig down through it. The other fact is the clear evidence that sod slicing was within the capacity of Neolithic man, equipped only with tools of wood

PLATE 3

a Kearney's town, Lenan townland, County Donegal. Infield to right, outfield to left. (Photograph: D. McCourt.)

b Linear clachan and striped infield on coastal platform, Malin Beg, County Donegal. Former outfield, partly enclosed, and common grazing beyond. (Photograph: N.C. Mitchel.)

PLATE 4

A County Down landscape near Hillhall, Lagan Valley, showing scattered farms, irregular fields, and remains of rath (bottom right). (Photograph: N.C. Mitchel.)

and stone, for vast quantities of sods were incorporated in great funerary mounds such as New Grange in the Boyne valley. And we know that, as we shall see in the next Chapter, cultivation ridges of prehistoric antiquity have been found under several feet of blanket bog (pl. 1b).[23] Research now being undertaken on such sites should tell us whether the waterlogging which, by preventing the decay of plants, encouraged peat to accumulate on top of the mineral soil was brought about by climatic change or by human interference. Where climate and vegetation are critically balanced, even small changes on either side could tip the balance. It seems possible that we shall find different causes operating in different times and places. However this may be, it would seem that the narrow spade and the long-handled shovel, which have been the Irish navvy's passport overseas, have an ancestry of some forty centuries. Who can tell what profound consequences such aptitudes, an addiction to hand implements and to small-scale units of social and economic life, have had on the nature of the Irish countryman and of Irish society?

III

The Irish heritage

It is the geographer's belief that the nature of man's environment is a significant if frequently forgotten strand in the pattern of his culture, revealing itself in diverse and often unexpected ways. I propose in this chapter to pick out from the pattern of Irish culture some of the hidden threads which are rarely caught up in the net of written history, whether because they are beyond its chronological reach or because they concern the common people who by and large neither left records nor figure in them. I have chosen the term 'heritage' to cover this large segment of human history. I acknowledge that the word has emotional overtones, and that 'our heritage' is a phrase much mouthed nowadays by evangelical politicians. Undeterred, I am using it in the sense which I gave it in a little book, *Irish Heritage*, written thirty years ago: it comes close to the dictionary definition as 'anything unrecorded which has been handed down', and with the help of 'habitat' and 'history' it conveniently provides me with an alliterative title.

The famous compiler of an earlier dictionary, Dr Johnson, put on record his view that all that was not written about the past was unknowable, but since his day the hard capsule of a literary monopoly in the study of the past has been broken. Even such an incapsulated scholar as F.R. Leavis has reminded us that a literary education is a substitute for traditional ways of speech and life soaked in immemorial experience and adjustment to the environment and the yearly rhythm of nature.[1] A great variety of methods and tools for investigating the unwritten past has been devised, and a battery of new techniques has come to the aid of archaeological excavation, including pollen analysis, C14 dating, dendrochronology and air photography. The collection of legends, myths and bygones has given way to the scientific classification of folk tales and the ethnological interpretation of folk crafts, customs and beliefs. To this we must add comparative linguistics and dialect studies, and – of particular interest to the geographer and the archaeologist – field observation, on foot and from the air, of relics in the cultural landscape, of old fences and field-systems, abondoned habitations, trackways and other artefacts, and their elucidation by comparative and distributional studies. I may instance what has come to be called 'hedgerow history', which claims to be able to date enclosure by counting the number of plant species in a hedgerow, working on the tested hypothesis that they increase at the rate of one a century.[2] (The Danes, similarly, have a method of dating field-walls, relating successive accretions to periods of field clearance.) It is not a method we would find of much use in Ireland, not only because hedgerows of any age are rare in most parts of the country, but also because I would not expect English logic to apply to Irish hedges. One is reminded, however, of F.W. Maitland's prescient reference to 'the testimony of our fields and walls and hedges'. It was Maitland, too, who referred to the ordnance map as 'a marvellous palimpsest, which under Dr Meitzen's guidance we are beginning to decipher'.[3] August Meitzen, it may be recalled, in his monumental researches on European field-systems and rural settlements published towards the end of last century, was working in the tradition of Humboldt and Ritter, and if his Teutonic search for ethnic explanations of habits of single-farm and nucleated settlement (Einzelhof and Gewanndorf) was to prove profitless (he thought they were respectively and uniquely of Celtic and Germanic origin), this does not detract from the value of the vast collection of comparative material he assembled.

It was another German scholar, J.C. Zeuss, who, claiming to have solved the problem of the Celtic languages,[4] envisaged the Celts as 'a vast pastoral race overrunning Europe' and thus gave encouragement to fervid Irish Nationalists to think of themselves as Celts. It might be supposed that Celtic scholars, if only in reaction against Germanic theory, would not be led astray by confusing race with language or any other cultural feature. Yet not only politicians and journalists but historians, linguists and perhaps geographers too have been known to refer to the Irish as a Celtic race because they once spoke Gaelic. Logically then, one should now call them English because they speak English. It can readily be demonstrated that language and race cannot be equated; for example, a Gaeltacht Irishmen who has abandoned Gaelic for English does not change his physique. Supposing that such a thing as a pure Celtic race ever existed, and that, however improbably, it achieved a mass invasion of Ireland, if it still exists as a distinct race it would have had to exterminate a native population which had been established for over 5000 years, and which would have found a thousand refuges in mountain, forest and bog. We would have to ignore also a very large infusion of English and other alien blood since the Middle Ages. It would seem rather that, as a late and marginal episode in the Celtic expansion from Central Europe, successive bands of warriors who spoke some kind of Celtic tongue, reaching Ireland probably from the late Bronze Age onwards, established themselves as conquering castes. They doubtless had their camp followers of various breeds. In the course of time the Celtic tongue was adopted by the bulk of the population just as it was later adopted by other settlers who had spoken Norse, French, English or Welsh, for example. Yet we are asked to regard this mongrel collection of people as a Celtic race. I use the word mongrel advisedly, and as a compliment, not a term of abuse. It seems that the ideas which a nationalistic society, on the European model, has about its past are not only most dangerous when they are erroneous, but also most powerful. The concept of pure races has long been rejected by anthropologists, who think of human types as conveyors of bundles of heritages which are re-combined in every generation. We should abandon, as Robin Flower suggested, the vain search for the pure uncontaminated Celt. If it were possible to sort out the genes of the Irish people I would hazard a guess that those coming from English settlers would exceed those deriving from 'the Celts', and that those coming from older stocks would constitute the largest proportion.[5] The popular conception of race as an ideal quality which has somehow lost its purity seems to spring from the biblical story of the garden of Eden, and finds analogies in the grammarian's concept of an original 'common Celtic' and in the theories of the Grimm brothers on the origin of folk tales in a pure Indo-European cradle. The extension of these notions into the idealisation of Nordic man in Nazi Germany should be a warning.

It is more to the point to notice that, among the physical heritages which are strong in the people of Ireland, are large and moderately long heads and, particularly in the west and north, a relatively high proportion of blood group O, a feature which is characteristic also of Scotland, Iceland, the Basque country and the western Mediterranean region, that is its distribution is markedly peripheral in Europe – which generally has a relatively high A frequency, as has south-east England – and in a larger view is also peripheral in the Old World. Certain other distinctive regional characteristics, though as variations in the human species they may not be as long established as the blood group heritage, have been observed in Ireland; for example, the lightly pigmented eye occurs in over eighty per cent of the population, but, while this feature has been thought to be an adaptation to the cloudy skies of north-western Europe, in Ireland it is commonly combined with hair which shows no corresponding reduction of pigmentation. According to the findings of one anthropometric survey, the combination of very dark hair and blue eyes is most common in County Wexford, and stranger still, the Aran Islanders, popularly regarded as the purest of Gaels, have relatively high frequencies of blood group A, thanks, it is suggested, to Cromwell's garrison of Fensmen. It is less surprising that there are relatively high A frequencies in the population of eastern Ireland.[6] In summary, it can be said that anthropometric research gives us a picture of the Irish population which is far removed from the stereotypes of blonde invaders and black-a-vised natives. In particular it points to very considerable heritages from Neolithic farmers and from Mesolithic fisherfolk, the latter being strongest in the western peninsulas. But I do not wish to pursue the problem of race. Whatever virtue there may be in physical character seems to spring from cross-breeding rather than from any supposed purity of race, but this is not to deny that racial or facial forms may, for instance, have a bearing on pronunciation and therefore have cultural significance. We get a very restricted view of the Irish people by thinking of them as 'Celts', overlooking not only the productive mingling of many varieties of historic settlers but also the substantial contribution of older stocks who had peopled the land in pre-Celtic times and absorbed its nature. It is not only writers of popular history and political propaganda who pursue the Celtic myth. Some Celtic scholars have been guilty of the very crime with which they reproach English historians of medieval Ireland, of treating the country as though nothing of significance had happened there before. The history of early Celtic Ireland has been written in much the same imperialist spirit as that in which the history of Roman Britain used to be written, as though the natives were conscious of their inferiority and anxious to receive the benefits of civilisation. Prehistorians, however, are steadily revealing and re-evaluating the cultural variety and vitality of an older Ireland.

It is rewarding to look at the Gaelic language in the light of the abundant evidence for the survival of population from pre-Celtic times – in the light of the Irish heritage. As Professor David Greene has declared with patriotic pride: 'Irish is a language made in Ireland: it is neither Indo-European nor Celtic, Pictish or Hamitic, but simply the linguistic expression of the Irish people.'[7] The new language, it might be said, was poured into an Irish mould. Our Queen's University scholar, Professor Heinrich Wagner, has written: 'Insular Celtic, prior to its earliest literary periods, must have undergone revolutionary changes to become one of the most bizarre branches of Indo-European.'[8] One of the probable points of entry for Celtic-speaking people, to judge from the fame and sanctity they came to attach to the river and its venerable megalithic burial sites, was the river Boyne. As a Welshman I have often wondered, when listening to a Gaelic speaker, whether a megalithic mouth or a palaeolithic palate could have made the difference. Mr Brendan Adams suggests that, on analogy with other old Eurafrican languages, those spoken in pre-Celtic Ireland probably lacked a p-phoneme, and that this would have favoured the adoption of Q-Celtic rather than P-Celtic.[9] But of course it is not merely a matter of pronunciation. Professor Wagner points out, following up Professor Morris Jones' early work on comparative typology, that 'many peculiar features of Insular Celtic, rarely traceable in any other Indo-European language, have analogies in Basque, Berber, Egyptian, Semitic and even in Negro-African languages'.[10] We seem to be dealing with the peripheral relics of an Old World substratum. In the light of this interpretation, the old argument as to whether any Gael on his way to Ireland ever set foot in England, even if not politically motivated, becomes irrelevant. I have no competence in this field: what matters for a regional geographer is that grammatical and phonological changes appear to occur in a language when it takes over a particular geographical and social environment and is affected by contact with languages long spoken there. This need come as no surprise to students of Anglo-Irish dialects who recognise their hybrid nature, but it demonstrates the value of an anthropogeographic view of general history. The traditional literary approach to the study of language and grammar, as to other aspects of human culture, has been blind to much that is of scientific interest and interpretative value. Field study and the distributional mapping of dialect differences, as pursued in Ireland by Heinrich Wagner and Brendan Adams, bring linguistics in close touch with anthropogeography.

A similar approach to the interpretation of other aspects of Gaelic culture – to see it as Irish rather than Celtic – would be illuminating. Did the Celts conquer Ireland, or rather did Ireland conquer the Celts? This is not to deny the distinctive Celtic quality of the place-names and institutions of early historic Ireland, of her art, her oral literature and lyric poetry and her rich mythology, or to question the value of comparative studies which reveal many parallels with other peripheral cultures of the Indo-European world. The Celtic warriors, classical writers tell us, were known for their bellicosity and an addiction to alcohol and poetry – they seem to have gone together, for the warriors apparently went drunk into battle, 'loudly proclaiming their own valorous quality'[11] – and if these were Celtic attributes it cannot be denied that they are with us still. Celtic art, it has been said, owed its origin to Celtic thirst in so far as its motifs were borrowed from Greek and Etruscan designs on wine vessels imported into eastern France. In Ireland, wines came to be supplemented first by mead and later by whiskey. And if 'the most typical symbol of Celtic pagan religion was the cult of the severed head', the cult may be said to survive, for the field of scholarly enquiry into early Irish history, not least Patrician history, is littered, metaphorically, with severed heads.[12] But, however much historians differ, there has been a tacit understanding that the Celtic invasion was somehow 'good', presumably because it gave Ireland its Gaelic tongue and left a deep imprint on Irish Christianity. We have no record of what the natives felt about it. The Viking invasion on the other hand was 'bad': it came late enough for its misdeeds to be documented – though it must be admitted that the monkish chroniclers were not unbiassed – and although it is conceded that the Norsemen brought such mundane benefits as trading towns, markets and a coinage, one is likely to be accused of 'whitewashing' them if one stresses the point. The traditional view of the past as a series of events or accidents must emphasise change, whereas if we look at history against its background of habitat and heritage we must recognise that there was a large measure of continuity. Even such a striking innovation as the Celtic art of the warrior aristocracy quickly takes on a distinctive Irish flavour. Academic historians, too, working for the most part in prescribed periods and looking for institutional change, have found little to interest them in the underlying continuities, despite their avowed concern with the stream of time.

Some startling re-evaluations, however, have recently been made, for example by Dr A.T. Lucas, who claims that at least half the burnings and pillages of churches, from the seventh century to the sixteenth, were the work of the Irish themselves, and that this destructive habit began before the Norsemen came and lasted long after they were forgotten.[13] He might have added that it still goes on. Moreover, regional cultural differences seem to have been as strong in early Celtic and early Christian times as they were, to judge from many prehistoric distributions, long before. One has the impression from histories written not long ago that the idealistic model of a nationally united island had existed from time immemorial,[14] though the unfortunate bellicosity of Ulster, whether in pagan or Christian times, could not be denied. New cultures have entered Ireland most easily in the north, by the short sea route: those reaching the south had many possible entries and might come either from England or direct from the Continent. The north thus tended to form a distinct cultural region or group of regions, behind its frontier belt of drumlins and, if we can believe the heroic tales, its leaders – the Men of Ulster – were prepared to defend it to the end against the Men of Ireland. In the words attributed to the Ulster warriors: 'We will stand our ground though the earth should split under us and the sky above on us.'[15] Fragmentation, regional rivalries and the resultant tensions have contributed a great deal to the character of Ireland. Professor P.L. Henry refers to the difference between Ulster and the rest of Ireland as 'one of the most deeply-rooted, ancient, and – from a literary point of view – most productive facts of early Irish history'.[16]

I suggest that the Celtic overlay, whose traditions are here fortunately preserved in a great epic, only reinforced an older and persistent regional distinction, and that the other subdivisions of early Celtic Ireland probably have an anthropogeographic base. Gaelic culture as a whole, like the Gaelic language, seems to have taken shape by being poured into an Irish mould, a mould having varied regional designs. In the end it was the power and ceremonial prestige of the favoured region around Tara, which lies near the centre of the 'metropolitan' eastern lowlands, that was to prevail and claim an ephemeral high kingship in the tenth century (fig. 3). The archaeological evidence suggests that, in selecting the hill of Tara, the newcomers had deliberately taken over a site that had long been sacred; and traces of a similar continuity are being revealed by work on some of the other fortress palaces of the regional kings. Not only is the royal enclosure or hill-fort at Tara built around a passage grave mound, but as we have seen, the river Boyne and its majestic megalithic graves, erected nearly two millennia before the grand assemblage of Celtic monuments was constructed at Tara, occupied a special place in Gaelic mythology. Thanks to the recent spectacular discoveries of Dr George Eogan the great mound of Knowth stands revealed as the greatest con-course of megalithic art in Europe (pl. 2), and it was chosen as a Celtic citadel. The Boyne was probably the main point of entry for the band of Celtic warriors who occupied Meath, and in respecting the sanctity of the monuments of earlier cultures they were in a strong position to extend their conquests. One suspects that these warriors with their memories of continental landscapes were fascinated by this strange world much as German visitors in our own day feel the magic of the Irish west. At any rate the vitality of native beliefs seems to have been renewed under new masters.

In this environment with its visible megalithic heritage the Celtic pre-occupation with the other-world was surely strengthened. Similarly, it is difficult to believe that the immense store of lore and custom associated with festivals such as Lughnasa, occurring at the beginning of autumn, or 'harvest', whose present-day survivals, including the ever popular pilgrimage to the rocky summit of Croagh Patrick, have been brilliantly documented and interpreted by Maire MacNeill,[17] do not contain a large pre-Celtic element, particularly where they concern high hilltops and rivers and lakes. Wakes for the dead, fairy-lore and animal-lore also seem to have ancient roots. In this Atlantic environment, a grazier's paradise, cattle came to be the main source of wealth and prestige; and the theme of the greatest epic tale of the Gaels is a cattle raid. In the vast body of customs and beliefs concerning cattle which have been transmitted orally are certain strange practices such as 'blowing' cows to induce a flow of milk, and bleeding them for food, which find parallels in North Africa, Western Asia and the ancient East[18] and which may go back to a prehistoric substratum to which anthropological and linguistic evidence appears to point. It is difficult to see them as other than pre-Celtic.

Because of the apparent speed with which a Celtic language took posses-sion of Ireland in the early Iron Age some students prefer to look to a much earlier period, for example the early Bronze Age, for the first adop-tion of a Celtic or at least some related Indo-European language. Certainly the Bronze Age was a time of cultural blossoming in Ireland, literally its Golden Age, thanks partly to its possession of native copper and gold. It cannot be denied that trade in metals and metal goods brought connections with Central Europe, the 'Celtic cradle', and indeed, trade alone might have been sufficient to account for the spread of a new vocabulary if not of a new language in a pre-literate society. It was in the Bronze Age that the Europe of history is first foreshadowed as a cultural unit, as is illustrated, for example, by a distribution map of flange-hilted bronze swords. Similarly it was in the course of a lengthy Bronze Age (occupying most of the last two millennia B.C.) that a uniform technology and standardised artefacts – always allowing for minor regional differences – were first established throughout Ireland. Since copper and tin rarely occur together in nature and must be assembled to produce the alloy, there was a quickening of trade and commercial contacts. It seems, indeed, that those parts of the world that have lacked the experience and the apprenticeship of a Bronze Age were slow to advance towards civilisation. It was in the early days of metal that the last and most numerous of all Irish megalithic tomb types (the wedge grave, a distinctive form of which nearly 400 examples survive) spread through the four provinces as the first all-Irish grave form.[19] Introduced apparently from north-west France, the wedge graves have one of their main concentrations in west Cork, a region rich in copper which, lacking ready supplies of flint, had been remote and thinly peopled in Neolithic times. They appear to have been the cultural trade mark of pastoral prospecting and trading groups who sought the hills where the pastures and scrub of Neolithic clearings were available and where metals might be found. The south-west, after an early production of copper axes, evidently exported its copper, for few bronzes have turned up there. An exception is a type of bronze horn belonging to the late Bronze Age: the only other part of Ireland where such horns (in fact a variant type) have been found in any numbers is Ulster.[20] (It was on the strength of these horns that a German archaeologist pronounced that 'the ancient Irish excelled in wind music'!) Earlier in the Bronze Age these two peninsular areas had variant types of ritual stone circles, a feature which is rare in other parts of Ireland but which characterises a number of areas in the pastoral north-western fringe of Europe where diverse cultures came together.

The 'wedge folk' moving north met in Ulster those better-known pastoral trading rovers and bowmen, the eager beaker-folk. Reaching Ireland from north Britain, they have been regarded by some archaeologists and by one or two linguistic scholars as the first Celtic-speaking Irishmen. Early forms of their characteristic copper and bronze daggers are rare in Ireland outside Ulster, but a type of ritual weapon of Central European origin which was eagerly adopted somewhat later to become a distinctive Irish artefact, the halberd, is well distributed throughout the island. Of the four types of the European beaker which have been found in Ireland to date, four were brought from north Britain to the northern half of Ireland, to Ulster and the Boyne entry, and one came into the south-west, together with copper-working, from the middle Rhinelands.[21] Throughout the earlier Bronze Age new ceramic types entered the country in the north-east, diffusing through most of the country as did successive types of bronze axes and other implements, of which several thousands have been found.[22] The north-east, with its multiple contacts, stands out as an area of innovation, shown for example in a concentration of highly decorated bronze axes which were exported to Britain and beyond. That there was at the same time an inheritance of cultural capital and a strong element of continuity is suggested by the continued occupation of long-favoured areas of sand and gravel and of the coastal sandhills. Continuity is apparent also in the persistence of hilltop burial. The most characteristic relics of the Bronze Age in all parts of the country are the hilltop cairns, at once monumental evidence of man's faith and aspirations and enduring landmarks striding through time and linking the cultural landscapes of past and present.

While the technical novelties and the prestige associated with the first metal workers probably resulted in some linguistic change, it seems more likely, on archaeological as well as linguistic grounds,[23] that it was the late Bronze Age that brought the earliest Celtic tongue to Ireland and an iron technology that ensured its victory. It can be shown from the distribution and typology of their field monuments and artefacts that the invaders reached Ireland by two main routes, from Britain via the east and north-east, and from the Continent via the south. The chief cultural division that arose was between north and south, renewing and perpetuating differences of outlook that had existed in earlier times. The many innovations of the Iron Age – and especially the widespread availability of bog iron ore as a source for the new metal – would explain the apparent speed with which a new language in association with new institutions and a novel technology was adopted in Ireland. It is not necessary to invoke mass invasion to explain cultural change, as the solitary figure of Saint Patrick, or even two or three Patricks, should remind us. Though not all the items in what would have been a formidable complex of material culture have as yet been attested in the Irish early Iron Age, the list probably includes oats, rye and flax, rotary querns, harrows, iron tools such as axes, iron-shod implements such as ploughs and spades, and horse-drawn wheeled vehicles: the celebrated Irish chariot itself was apparently not far removed from a dung-cart,[24] though it must be admitted that there is almost no archaeological evidence of either vehicle. Add to this complex the aristocratic novelty of isolated homesteads, the circular earth or stone-ringed raths and cashels of which some 30,000 can still be traced (fig. 7 and pl. 4); add also the lake-dwellings (crannogs), which, whatever their origins, began to proliferate in the succeeding centuries: graft the whole on to a long established stock and you have the material essentials of a rural society which persisted in many areas into the seventeenth century, and of which traces have remained into our own time. This archaic form of society was organised in numerous small kingdoms related to topographic units and grazing capacities.

It is worth expanding the brief reference to oats, for they were to become the Irish corn and to play a significant part in the agricultural pattern as in the food and folklife of the country. Like rye, oats made their first

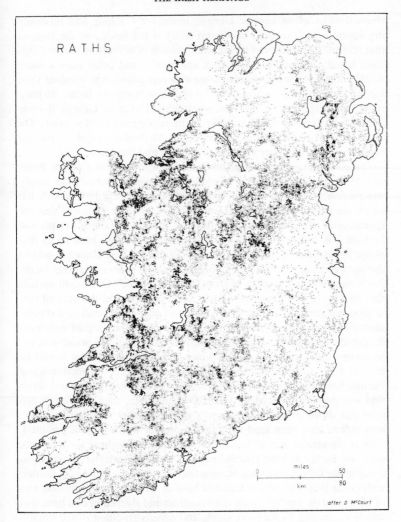

RATHS

Fig. 7. Distribution of enclosed farmsteads (raths) covering approximately the first millennium A.D. (After D. McCourt.)

appearance as a cultivated crop in the European Bronze Age, when ancestral weeds took over fields of barley and wheat in environments where acid soils and wet summers did not favour the older crops. Less demanding than wheat and more tolerant of humid conditions, they also fitted more comfortably into a pastoral setting, providing fodder for favoured livestock while also helping to 'support the people'. One of the

51

characteristics of an oceanic climate, moreover – a long and relatively dry spring – has favoured maximum effort in the fields and the bogs at that season. Being sown in spring, the problem of protecting winter crops from hungry animals did not arise, and in this and other ways a more flexible and much less elaborate scheme of regulations was required than for the cultivation of wheat. The English Establishment found its deep roots and prejudices in the rich wheatfields. Listen to George Borrow fulminating in Wild Wales as he trod the rocky road to Holyhead: 'On my right was a field of oats; on my left a Methodist chapel – oats and Methodism! What better symbols of poverty and meanness!'

The good luck associated in folk tradition with particular plants, crops and livestock is a matter of ecological experience rather than empty superstition. Oats and cattle, for instance, are closely linked with the hazel, the whitethorn and the rowan. I have elsewhere suggested that the superstitious veneration in which the lone thorn – the thorn not planted by man – is still held in many parts of Ireland may go back to its first magic appearance at the sun-lit edge of Neolithic forest clearings, and to the early observation that its bounteous blossoms were a sign that heavy frosts were over and supplies of fresh fodder assured.[25] Oral tradition tells that oats could be successfully grown wherever the hazel throve, and that 'a good nut year was a good oat year'. Hazel nuts long remained a supplementary source of food, and years blessed with a great crop of nuts were frequently recorded, for example, in the Annals of Inisfallen, which purport to cover events from the earliest times. While the Mesolithic would be beyond their furthest reach, it is worth noting that in north-western Europe generally many mesolithic sites are associated with hazel scrub that was perhaps induced by firing. Our ancestors, then, in times when food ran short, if not like the poet's primitive man 'loud with acorns', may indeed have been loud with nuts and other wild vegetable products.

Over the greater part of Ireland the preference for spring sown cereals, oats and barley, is long established, and if today barley is favoured, as it was in the Bronze Age, oats became the historic Irish corn. In association with cattle they formed the material base of a rather rough, restless way of life, based on kinship rather than contract and steeped in oral lore, that stands in contrast to the more stable and orderly tradition of the English lowlands, which with its market towns, villages and openfields was introduced by the Anglo-Normans into parts of eastern and southern Ireland. The heavy mould-board plough, calling for co-operation and team work, was adapted to fairly level stretches of good soil, where two, three or four openfields surrounding the village settlement could be most conveniently ploughed in long strips or acres roughly corresponding to a days' work, a furrow-long (220 yards) and a chain (22 yards) in width. Fertility was maintained by keeping one field fallow in rotation, and a seasonal schedule of customary laws governed the villagers' rights and duties under the authority of a resident squire. Behind it we may see the obligations of gifts and services given to rural leaders in prehistoric Europe which were, for Marc Bloch, the beginnings of feudalism. The rectangular timber houses which had been characteristic of Central and Western Europe from the Neolithic often came to be grouped around an open green as villages grew in size. The leisurely game of cricket seems to have had its origins in the English village green and to have taken its pitch of twenty-two yards from the measure of a plough strip; and with its stratified teams of gentlemen and players it is a fitting symbol of the English low-lands. The geographical and social distribution of the game in Ireland is a fair index of English influence – in cricket language, of the 'Gentlemen of Ireland'. To the Irishman whose more vigorous sports such as hurling belong to the rough ridged outfield rather than to the smooth village green, cricket is a matter for jest and a sign of simple-minded Englishry.

In Gaelic Ireland, settlement and society developed differently. The single-farm unit which is so conspicuous in the Irish landscape today is in origin at least as old as the early Celtic period, and in theory this is the settlement form best suited to the needs of a society dependent on a pastoral economy and closely attached, with magical as well as practical purpose, to livestock. The well-being and fertility of the cattle were linked to those of the family. It was this attitude and this cultural pattern, rather than sheer poverty – the only conceivable explanation for the Englishman – that allowed the unhygienic habit of living with animals to persist. It was reported of County Tyrone at the beginning of last century that 'one house answers for the family and the cow for more than one-third of the peasantry',[26] and even in 1841 nearly half the houses in Donegal had one room only (fig. 8). In 1847 that remarkable and surely truthful Quaker traveller, Asenach Nicholson, describing the house of the handsome lady who was one of the two owners of Omey Island in County Galway, states that, in the kitchen, she 'counted sixty-three living and moving beings, not counting humans'.[27]

There is no incontrovertible evidence for the existence of the single-farm system in pre-Celtic Ireland, but both literary and archaeological evidence show that the raths, cashels and crannogs of the Gaels were the isolated homes of chieftains and freemen. Where then did the peasantry live? Neither history nor archaeology furnishes us with much evidence, but working back from the recent past we can say that the traditional unit of settlement accompanying the rundale or infield/outfield system, mentioned in the last chapter, was the hamlet or kin-cluster. Both clustered settlements and some kind of infield/outfield agriculture have their historic parallels in Highland Celtic Britain, and these cultural traits have accordingly been labelled Celtic, despite the warning of Meitzen's ethnic errors. Like so much else that is loosely called Celtic, it can best be understood in terms of the physical and social environment of those parts of the British

53

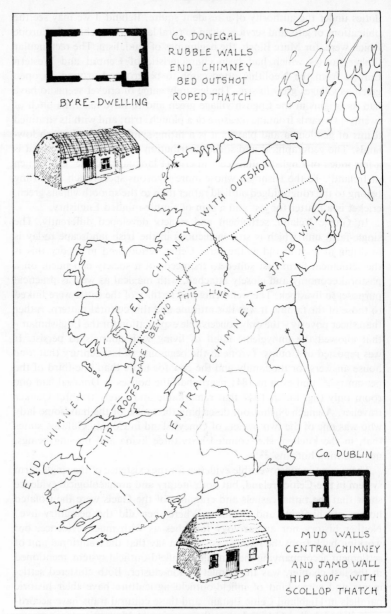

Fig. 8. Traditional peasant house types.

Isles which retained the Celtic languages. However this may be, its nature has had far-reaching consequences in history. Much of the country has lacked the civilising experience of true village life.

Text-books until recently have stated that Ireland had *always* been a land of isolated holdings, however unlikely this seems in the light of comparative anthropology. In fact, there is abundant evidence for the widespread occurrence of small villages or hamlets (clachans) associated with an openfield system (rundale or infield/outfield) in the eighteenth and nineteenth centuries, especially in the decades before the Great Famine. Its dissolution was mostly the work of landlords and required no Enclosure Acts: otherwise it would surely have attracted more attention from economic historians. There are, it is true, many references to the system in travellers' accounts of Ireland, in the statistical surveys promoted by the Royal Dublin Society at the beginning of the last century, and in government reports, but historians had taken little notice of them, and it was not until geographical field observation had revealed relics of the system in operation that research into its historical geography was undertaken. It is one of the attributes of a society whose primary interests are pastoral that it can function without written contracts and records and therefore finds little place in documentary history. I recall my astonishment when, thirty-five years ago, I came across many modified but working examples of rundale communities in Gweedore, County Donegal; and they can still be found in a few localities in some parts of the country, including Northern Ireland. When I published my first paper on the subject[28] it was met with incredulity, and indeed very little was then known even about the 'English' openfields of Anglo-Norman Ireland.[29] I have included as an appendix a summary of one of the fullest descriptions ever written of the rundale system, compiled by Lord George Hill of Gweedore in 1845, which has long been out of print. It was this pamphlet, *Facts from Gweedore* that led me to the area in 1938, and it is a measure of the tenacity of the system that it still lingers there today although Hill claimed to have abolished it.

The best clue to the distribution of rundale in the early nineteenth century is to be found in the distribution of clachans as marked, in the form of house clusters, on the first Ordnance Survey maps (1832–40).[30] The correspondence is not exact because a few clusters have different origins and some of them had outlived the land system which brought them into being, but the general picture is clear (fig. 9). The clachans, consisting in general of 10–20 houses, though occasionally much larger, were located most typically in peripheral regions, especially in the west and north, but there were also strong concentrations in the south-east and in some east coast peninsulas such as Lecale in County Down and Forth in County Wexford. Such a peripheral distribution suggests that the clachan was a residual settlement type. While one would expect it to be restricted

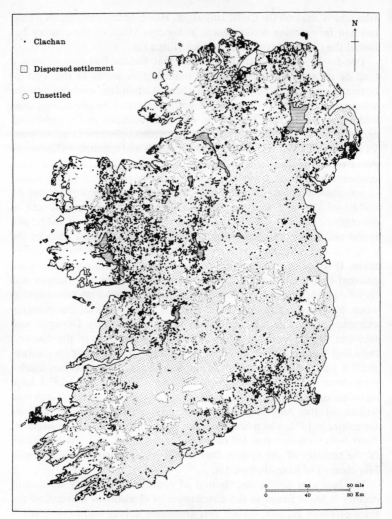

Fig. 9. Types of rural settlement, 1832–40. (After D. McCourt.)

to areas untouched by the Anglo-Normans, its occurrence in some of the eastern coastlands may be explained by the fact that the *betaghs* or unfree tenants in Anglo-Norman Ireland were allowed to live native-fashion, dwelling in family groups in their own townlands, In Lecale, in Anglo-Norman Ulster, a number of surviving clachans were still associated with a modified rundale system at the end of last century,[31] and less surprisingly both features were found on the fringes of the Wicklow

56

Mountains into the present century. The larger 'English' openfields of the Leinster lowlands were enclosed for the most part in the eighteenth century in the course of the agrarian revolution.[32] While some of the associated manorial villages survive, for the most part separate farms were built on the new compact holdings. Many areas of cleared woodland, of common pasture, reclaimed bog and mountain land were also enclosed in a regular pattern of five- to ten-acre fields. Isolated farms had been established earlier in some parts of Ireland during the Tudor and Cromwellian plantations, and in particular those parts of Ulster settled under James I had many single farms in the seventeenth century, but it was not until the nineteenth century that most of the peripheral areas and the hill margins throughout the country, that is the landscapes which are commonly regarded as most typical of Ireland, came to be dotted with the lone steadings which, our textbooks have told us, have characterised Ireland since time immemorial.

It is possible to reconcile these views if we bear in mind that written history, whether English or Gaelic, has concerned itself for the most part with the élites; and Ireland has had more than its share of them. It would be difficult to find a more rigid example of a simple caste system than that of nineteenth century rural Ireland with its landlords and peasants, reflected in the landscape in the big house with its high-walled wooded demesne and the naked countryside with its teeming tenantry. Gaelic society was organised very differently (the term 'tribal' is open to objections but Dr Binchy admits he knows of no better translation of the word *túath*)[33] but it was certainly aristocratic and hierarchical, 'a society more or less rigidly stratified and in which the inequality of man – based on differences of birth and calling – had been erected into a legal principle'. It is clear from the Irish laws that the aristocracy lived in raths of graded dimensions, from the tribal kings who traced their descent from ancestral deities and who were identified with the fertility of land, livestock and people, to the noblemen and their clients who seem to have been the equivalent of the landlords and the 'strong farmers' of recent times. Tens of thousands of their ringed raths survive in the countryside, preserved partly by superstition and partly because their deep-dug trenches are difficult to obliterate. Excavation has shown that they normally contain a single house and a single hearth. If the number of known raths seems excessive in relation to the probable number of nobles and freemen, it must be remembered that though the timber houses were reconstructed periodically they had a relatively short life and that raths were being built through a period of some 1,500 years, even if the majority of excavated examples dates from the early centuries of Christianity.

From a geographical point of view a major contribution of the rath-builders to the making of Ireland and the Irish landscape was the occupation of lowland areas of heavy soils and heavy forests, such as the drumlin belt, filling in the gaps between the long-occupied uplands and completing the film of population over the face of the land. Occasionally the remains of small field enclosures adjacent to and apparently contemporaneous with the raths have been observed on the ground and all the indications are that they were family farms. The Irish laws tell us, however, that the kin group of four generations (*fine*) was the normal property-owning unit, and it is not clear how this can be reconciled with the scattered distribution of the raths: it is exceptional to find two or three raths side by side. It may be that each rath was the home of an extended family. One remembers the crowded conditions which the Irish, for example the lady of Omey Island mentioned earlier, could apparently endure if not enjoy in the nineteenth century. Comfort was not high in the list of priorities. Or further study may show that there were undefended habitations of kinsmen adjacent to the raths. Despite the insistence of the laws on the rights of private property there are many references to open country (openfields?), to cultivation ridges and co-aration, and to temporary fences as well as stone walls. It is clear that the dominant interest of the rath-dwellers was in livestock – enormous quantities of animal bones have been recovered in excavations – and the paucity of domestic pottery on most sites, save in the north-east of the country, suggests that meat was a major item in the diet. The underground caves (souterrains) which are frequently associated with them were probably used for the storage of meat and milk products. But it would be wrong to suppose that cultivation was neglected: 'it was an economy in which a relatively well-developed system of tillage played an essential and conspicuous part.'[34] Ploughshares and other tools of cultivation are occasionally found in the raths, and querns are abundant.

Some scholars, notably F. Seebohm and H.L. Gray, have attempted to relate the evidence of the old laws to the rundale system and to the map evidence of townlands, quarterlands and other territorial divisions, but new interpretations of the old Irish law tracts are badly needed. The subject is an open field for co-aration by historians, legal experts, Celticists, anthropologists, archaeologists and geographers, but they have been slow to co-operate. Can the egalitarian rundale-clachan system as we know it from recent survivals be a degraded form of the land-holding system practised by the rath-dwelling grades of nobility described in legalistic terms for early Christian Ireland? Or should we think of it rather as deriving from a scheme of land-use associated with the lower grades and the unfree elements of the population of Gaelic Ireland? Some references in the laws suggest that the bondmen lived in clusters, had joint tenancies and practised joint cultivation, subdividing their openfield plots among co-heirs, and paying food rents as well as services of various kinds to the nobles. As we have seen, something similar was found among the *betaghs* of Anglo-Norman times. One of the obstacles to fuller understanding has been a reluctance in Ireland to see Gaelic society as evolving from the adjustment of a conquering aristocracy to a novel and difficult environment occupied by an obstinate and strongly conservative native population. In many parts of the country, especially among the hills, these would probably have far outnumbered the newcomers. The popular conception of the Gael as a noble creature – every Irishman's ancestor – living in splendid isolation relieved by grand periodic assemblies seems to be the joint product of the national revival and of the Romantic movement, for emancipation and nationalism gathered strength in the romantic ambience of the nineteenth century. (The Roman Catholic revival, similarly, was deeply coloured by the puritanism of early Victorian times.) Accordingly there has been a reluctance to admit that there was anything tribal or communal about the arrangements of Gaelic society: in the words of Professor Duignan, 'it was an economy grounded in private property in land and livestock'. This attitude was strengthened by the unfortunate statement made not long ago in a standard scholarly English work, 'that fifteenth century Ireland remained, in great part, a country of wandering pastoralists'.[35] Many Irishmen found this not very different from the verdict of Giraldus Cambrensis: 'they live on beasts only, and live like beasts'.[36] On the other hand the notion that the ancient Irish were free of the taint of communal practices breaks down in the light of comparative evidence from rural societies in many parts of the world. And in the course of centuries of English landlordism many families of proud descent, even if they had once enjoyed 'private property', were forced to join the ranks of the peasantry.

Neither history nor archaeology has thrown much light on or indeed taken much interest in the ancestry of the rundale system. When it is not ignored by academic historians one has the impression that it is regarded as a peculiar, perverse and malign response to the evils of landlordism and political manipulation in the seventeenth century, which grew to epidemic proportions from the middle of the following century with the correlated increase of potato-growing and population. Even in its decay, the field study of rundale as a functioning system set against its physical and social environment has added a new dimension to our understanding.[37] It was a system well adapted to the constraints of an uncertain climate and a difficult fragmented environment where good arable land was scarce but rough grazing plentiful in mountain and bog. Intensive use was made of a selected stretch of land, the infield, which might be on a well-drained hillside, an esker, or an old beach or a coastal or river terrace. Because crops were restricted to those sown in spring, and thanks to a ready supply of animal manure partly contributed by wintering livestock, the infield could be kept in more or less permanent cultivation and could, therefore, be worked with a light plough and simple gear: indeed, as we have seen it was sometimes pulled by the horse's tail. The plots were very small, however, and spade cultivation was more efficient. The Irish spade, in a great variety of shapes adapted to different soil conditions, was a narrow one-eared spade which can be closely paralleled in medieval England.[38] Rundale was much simpler and more flexible than the three field system, requiring less equipment and less organisation. It was egalitarian, and could operate without the benefit of a landlord, but it was complicated by the subdivision among co-heirs and in former times by the periodic reallocation of the holdings, which were scattered in many small plots so that all shared land of varying quality. Their reallocation was the occasion for noisy and prolonged disputes. The word used to describe the confusion of innumerable scattered plots and tortuous access ways in the infield was 'throughother', a word which has often been applied to other aspects of Irish life. I have suggested that the attitudes engendered by this mode of land use have had profound consequences in history.[39] In those parts of the country where the Gaelic system survived longest, whether or not the land was formerly held in rundale, it is common to find holdings scattered in several portions. Such dismemberment is a serious problem particularly in parts of Connacht, where native freeholders down to the sixteenth century enjoyed the use of scattered portions of land that was owned by the kinship group to which they belonged. Dr Jean Graham's work on the evidence contained in seventeenth-century surveys of Connacht[40] is throwing a new light on the Gaelic system of landholding at that time, and by inference on that which may have obtained in the age of the raths.

Reference has been made to the settlement type, the clachan, associated with the rundale system, and we must now take a closer look at it. It was a formless cluster of small farm houses which may be compared to the Scottish 'farm town' (pl. 3a). Lacking such village attributes as church and public-house, it comprised the homes of a constantly changing number of related families (or, in large clachans, of groups of related families) and it too was thoroughly 'throughother', expanding or decaying with no conceived plan (fig. 11), though under English landlords clachans were sometimes sited or rebuilt along a road and acquired a certain linear order (pl. 3b). I shall say something about house types when I have returned from the outfield, which is an essential feature of the system as we know it. It comprised the rough grazing around the settlement, from which crops were taken by changing the cultivated area every two or three years and leaving the abandoned plots 'to rest', a method which suggests primitive shifting agriculture and which, with the introduction of cultivated grasses, gave way to the present ley system which is its logical successor. The outfield terminated in some cases at the townland boundary, beyond which, in hilly areas, stretched the common grazing, frequently shared by a number of townlands. Elsewhere, summer grazing was available in adjacent bogs, or the 'mountain' might be a few miles away, involving some form of transhumance or, to give it its Anglo-Irish name, booleying (*buailteachas*).[41] A mountain in Ireland is measured not by the irrelevant precision of a contour line, but by the extent of the grazing it provides. It is as much a term of cultural appraisal as an elevation, and because different sections of a group of hills were named after the lowland districts to which they were attached, it has been found necessary to invent a single collective name for some of the hill ranges.

When I first encountered a rundale community in Donegal I had a strong feeling that I was witnessing the final degraded phase of a complex of very ancient practices. I wrote that I was 'tempted to regard the open-field system as a survival from pre-Celtic times'. Improbable as it seems, there is now, as we shall see, some field evidence to support this wild surmise, though we know almost nothing of the long intervening period. Some years later I had a strange sensation when helping a Donegal peasant to reap his oats with a toothed sickle in a small plot of ground under cut-away bog. We worked among the fossil stumps of pine trees that had been smothered in prehistoric times by several feet of blanket peat, and I had the feeling that we were not the first to reap a harvest on that plot, that the land had been cultivated long ago, before the trees had grown. The whole scene 'exhaled an air of unbelievable eld'. I imagined we were in a forest clearing of the Bronze Age, using tools of bronze and flint, and that the wind which was helping to dry the tiny sheaves as we worked was a ghost wind blowing in the vanished tree-tops.[42] In fact, as was noted in the previous chapter, unmistakeable signs of cultivation have been found under peat in several parts of the north and west of the country, and field walls as well as traces of habitation – in one instance (Ballyglass, County Mayo) a rectangular timber house – have been found underneath megalithic tombs and can probably be dated somewhere in the third millennium. At Ballyglass buried lazy-beds were also found alongside.[43] An extensive series of dry stone walls under blanket peat is being excavated in County Mayo by Mr Séamas Caulfield, and not far away in Carrownaglogh townland Dr Michael Herity has recently found bundles of unmistakable cultivation ridges – the tell-tale lazy-beds (pl. 1*a*) – inside a walled enclosure of about four acres, the whole looking remarkably like an infield and believed from associated finds to be of early Bronze Age date, say 1500 B.C., though pollen and carbon 14 dating of the overlying peat is not yet available.[44] Habitations have not so far been located here, but a well-known Neolithic settlement excavated by Professor O'Riordain at Lough Gur in County Limerick consisted of a loose cluster of about a dozen houses, some circular and some rectangular in plan, looking remarkably like a clachan.[45] Similar house clusters associated with kin groups and usually with partible inheritance, ancient enclosure and some variety of infield/outfield have been recorded from many parts of the pastoral

Atlantic fringe from Norway to Galicia.[46] And in Norway as well as in Scotland and here and there in Wales the lazy-bed is also found. I have already described its ecological adjustment to the Atlantic environment, but with the new evidence of its great antiquity one may think of it as a relict feature and look further afield for possible parallels. It would take us too far afield to discuss the impressive bundles of potato ridges made with the foot plough in old pastures up to heights of 14,000 feet in Bolivia and Peru, which are so strikingly similar to the lazy-beds that it has even been suggested that the ridge came to Ireland with the potato![47] What I have in mind is the practice of mounding the soil in cultivation clearings in many parts of the tropical forest. I have wondered whether the lazy-bed had its origin in the scraping up of humus in the forest soils of prehistoric Europe before the coming of the plough. The sod ridge would then have been a transference adapted to the tough swards developed as the clearings became grazing lots. However this may be, there is no doubting the long ancestry of the cultivation ridge.

Another agrarian practice for which there is a presumption of continuity from early times, indeed from the very beginning of agriculture, is the use of fire in preparing the ground. 'Paring and burning' was a widespread custom in the eighteenth and nineteenth centuries. The supply of phosphates secured by burning the pared sods and spreading the ashes procured heavy yields of potatoes and cereals, but the benefits were short-term and the Irish Parliament passed several Acts to try to prevent the practice from 1743 onwards. Yet it persisted in many parts of the country and was of most benefit where mountain or bog was reclaimed for potatoes grown in lazy-beds for two or three years in succession before reverting to outfield. It cannot be disputed that paring and burning played a very important role in Ireland in the eighteenth and nineteenth centuries in enabling a rapidly expanding population to subsist by the more intensive exploitation of the existing arable ground and by the colonisation of previously uncultivated bog and mountain land.[48] The practice is documented from the early Middle Ages, and when one remembers that the clearance of forest or scrub by fire preparatory to cultivation is well attested in Neolithic times in northern Europe – and is still practised in parts of Scandinavia as well as throughout equatorial lands – we may probably see in this custom another deeply implanted habit deriving from the needs of the first farmers.

I turn from the remote past to consider one of the most distinctive and colourful elements in the traditional Irish landscape – the peasant house. Vidal de la Blache called the house 'one of the faithful signs of the mentality of the occupant'. It is also, because it often outlives the builder and is associated with ancestral values, a conserving and conservative element of material culture. The landlord's house, typically more or less Georgian in style because conditions were rarely settled enough before the eighteenth century for a fully domestic fashion to prevail, is fairly well documented and has had many historians, but it has been left to geographers and ethnographers to study and to see the significance of the small farmhouse and the cottar's cabin in social and cultural history. The first serious study of the Irish rural house was made by the Swede, Ake Campbell, who, though familiar with the more elaborate Swedish farmhouses, saw personality and quality in humble houses which most visitors to Ireland had dismissed as 'wretched hovels'. This is what he wrote in 1937: 'Lacking nearly every architectural consciousness and at the same time every kind of imported building material, the Irish peasant house never stands out in bold relief against its background but melts into it even as a tree or rock. Whenever the old building traditions are faithfully maintained its features are of a fine simplicity. The best Irish thatching gives the finest peasant roof in Europe.'[49]

Campbell made a simple division of Irish houses into those with a gable hearth and those with a central hearth, the former occurring in the north and west and the latter in the east and south, though, as with almost every kind of cultural distribution in Ireland, there are exceptions; for example, the gable house goes with the mountain massifs in the east, which were refuge areas. Within each division there are many minor variations, of roofing techniques for instance, adjusted to local climate and materials, which were always obtained on the spot, and there may be slight differences of ground plan which have a larger significance. The age-old relations of north and west Connacht with north and west Ulster, for example, are reflected in the distribution of the 'outshot house', a gable hearth house with a projecting bed wing in a side wall near the fire, a feature that recalls the bed alcove of old houses in western Scotland (fig. 8). If this provides a folk-cultural parallel to the historical links between western Scotland and north-west Ireland – illustrated, for example, in the Galloglass movements from the thirteenth century[50] – the central hearth house of the east and south seems to point to old English connections. It meets the outshot house along a line running from Glenarm to Galway. The former is a variant of the pastoralists' longhouse or byre house, originally a single room, which once had a widespread distribution in north-western Europe and is well attested, for example, in medieval England. The older houses are built on a sloping site, the cattle occupying, for reasons of hygiene and manure conservation, what is still called the lower end of the house, away from the fire, the sleeping place being towards the hearth gable and being given simple architectural expression in the bed outshot. This enlarged the living space around the hearth in a house which was necessarily of restricted width. In the traditional Irish house this space is always kept free and there is no central table. Until two or three centuries ago, when walls came to be built of stone rubble with clay mortar, they were constructed of flimsy or poor load-bearing materials such as wattle-and-daub, clay-and-straw, or sods, so that the distance that could be safely spanned without wall support dictated, in the absence of sophisticated roof trusses, the width of the house. Timber supports for the roof seem to have taken the form either of paired crucks or of forked uprights, supporting through purlins. The roof timbers, moreover, the most important members of the house in a wet and windy climate, came to be of sturdy bog timber by preference and often from necessity, and it was difficult to extract serviceable oak logs of any length. The width of the house, being the width of a single room, lay within the limits of about twelve to eighteen feet, and the dimensions of the larger byre houses are almost exactly those of the Neolithic long houses that have been excavated. The dimensions of the three Neolithic oblong houses excavated to date are: Lough Gur, 17 feet by 32 feet; Ballyglass, County Mayo, 18 feet by 30 feet; and Ballynagilly, County Tyrone, 18 feet by 22 feet, giving an average of 18 feet by 28 feet. A singled storied house, with walls the height of a man and no more than one room wide but often provided with a half loft and capable of being divided transversely and extended lengthwise, became a cultural fixation apparently at a very early date. It was bolstered by many superstitious beliefs and the apparently monotonous simplicity of the traditional rural house cannot be entirely attributed either to the repressive forces of an evil land system or to universal poverty.

Perversely, the central hearth houses which seem to have prevailed in the south and east of Ireland are in one respect more archaic than the longhouses: they have preserved the hip roof, a feature which is still commonly seen. The reason for its replacement by the upright gable in other parts of the country, where the fire was not in the centre of the house, seems to have been the need for a vertical attachment when wattled, stone or brick chimney flues were provided for the fire, a fashion which spread slowly from the sixteenth century but did not become general until the nineteenth. The central-hearth house as we know it today, with its screen or jamb-wall standing between the fire and the door, could not have been used to house animals – for a through passage between opposite doors is a feature of the byre house – and even earlier versions of the type would have been divided, if only by an open fire, into two parts, presumably one for living and one for sleeping. This suggests that, perhaps from late medieval times, English standards of comfort were adopted.[51]

But if the south and east thus came to have a different house type, the essential dimensions of the smaller rural house did not change, though in the lowlands clay was frequently used for the walls (instead of stones) in place of the wattles and sods of earlier times. An almost universal feature, which was bound up with the stripping of sods as an agricultural practice, was the use of sods as underthatch. The internal arrangements of the living room, the sturdy functional forms of furniture, the open oven-less hearth with its crane and suspended round bottomed pots, the peasant stews and stirabouts and the gritty oaten thin-bread baked on a griddle and well greased with milk products, the disposition of the furnishings around and in the walls, leaving free the cooking, working and dozing place in front of the fire, the ever-open door or half-door on which one can lean and dream and which is kept open because it was once the only source of light – these and many other cultural traits, varying slightly from one district to another in a mosaic of ecological and historical diversities, were part of a far western heritage, poor in material resources but rich in spiritual values, resisting change and worshipping other things than progress, that was shared with many other parts of the Atlantic fringe of Europe.[52] All this, I suggest, has been for the majority of Irish people through the ages a cultural environment which lowland England was never able fully to understand or come to terms with.

IV

The personality of Ireland

In making my theme the personality of a country, my younger geographical critics will say that I am merely demonstrating the survival in Ireland of an old-fashioned concept and an outmoded vocabulary, that I too am living in the past. It cannot be denied that Ireland clings to the past, but I would challenge the notion that to be 'relevant' and 'predictive' one must confine one's attention to the present. I have already briefly traced the history of the concept of geographical personality. I would add that its greatest living exponent, in another far western land, is Professor Carl Sauer of the University of California, Berkeley, and I commend his essay on 'The Personality of Mexico'. It is from a retro-spective science, he says, that the ability to look ahead can be acquired. For him the term 'embraces the whole dynamic relation of life and land', and his conclusion bears some resemblance to the conclusion I must draw: 'in that antithesis (between north and south), which at times means conflict and at others a complementing of qualities, lie the strength and weakness, the tension and harmony that make the personality of Mexico'.[1] A few archaeologists in Britain, following Sir Cyril Fox, have also adopted the term,[2] but for anthropologists, regional personality has come to mean the nature of individual personalities taken as representative of particular cultures or regions.[3]

It is perhaps in this sense that many Irish people would interpret my title, for although most Irish literature has little geographical content and even books entitled 'Ireland' may tell us almost nothing about the land itself, the personification of the country has been a persistent theme, and it has taken the form of female figures who were originally deities, wishful symbols of the fertility of the land and the people. Dark Rosaleen and Kathleen ni Houlihan are the Anglo-Irish versions.[4] But there was, too, a sense of geographical personality in the older Irish literature, a sense of the harmony and mystery of man's place in nature. The gods dwelt among the hills, and the living spirits of the land were ever present. One genre of Gaelic writing concerned itself with the preservation of a great store of oral traditions relating to places, and especially to hills. The collected stories, the Dindshencas, has been called an Irish Dictionary of National Topography.[5] Moreover, a pagan sense of communion with all living things runs through the ancient tales and inspires some out-standing lyric poetry. While a sense of a timeless bond between man and nature is apparent in much modern Irish poetry, it would be difficult, and beyond my competence, to demonstrate that there has been continuity from the pagan past. But I think it would be fair to say that the Christian interlude turned men's thought away from nature. Although Professor Greene has reminded us that Irish monks were much given to the pagan custom of composing nature poems in the vernacular,[6] contemplation of the physical world and its beauty appears to have been regarded as a dangerous activity, and certainly Christian dogma must have discouraged a search for origins which, though it may and perhaps must be fruitless, is intellectually stimulating and has sound Aristotelian precedents. The classic Christian tradition which is our academic heritage tended to isolate man from nature, to separate the humanities from the sciences and to see human thought and action as the moving forces and the only final cause of history. Some historians, I suspect, would see in the title of this lecture a reference to the Great Men of Irish history whose personalities they evaluate, whose motives they somehow divine, and whose memory they seek to preserve, despite the dangerous passions their very names arouse on one side or the other. To avoid any of these alternative inter-pretations I might have called these lectures The Character of Ireland, but I was not encouraged by the contents of a composite work on *The Charac-ter of England*, edited by Sir Ernest Barker, which almost ignores England.[7] This volume of 575 pages, which is full of admirable learning, devotes less than thirty pages to what I have called habitat and heritage.

It will be clear by now, I hope, that my view of history is that of Marc Bloch, for whom land life and history were inseparable. Let me illustrate this approach to history by looking briefly at the environment and life of Russia, and contrasting its vast continental monotony and climatic extremes with the insular diversity and climatic monotony of Ireland. The differences in society, economy and political history are as clear as those in environment and in scale, yet because they are both locationally mar-ginal to the full European experience, one can make certain comparisons be-tween these two ends of Europe as regions of difficulty and survival. Looked at geographically, the nation state, a product of Western Europe, seems to have been most successful where it had the advantage of a fairly clearly defined and defensible core or heartland such as the Ile de France, out of which, by the absorption of neighbouring regions, normally but not necessarily of like speech, larger political units emerged, combining more or less successfully, with adjustments of policy and often of frontiers, ancestral diversities. A common environmental factor in the early growth of these units seems to have been their location in a lowland basin of well-drained brown earths with no extremes of climate, capable of yielding a good surplus of cereals and other food products and providing a base for the growth of feudalism. In contrast, the Mediterranean lands are weak in territorial bases but have repeatedly, and from far earlier times, ex-pressed their personality in the city state. Geographers have long taken the bounteous olive tree as a reliable index of Mediterranean climate and culture. If one were to choose the best natural index of the brown earths and moderate climates of Western Europe it would not be the regal oak, which likes heavier soils, but that queen of deciduous trees, the delicate-leaved beech; and it is of interest that the natural limits of the beech fall short of Ireland in the west, and of Russia in the east. We may not agree with Toynbee's judgement that 'the Irish are a byword for their prolonged failure to create an effective united Irish state'[8] – and, if we do, we will find a dozen different explanations – but most of us will agree that the Russians have had persistent problems of political organisation and stability and have sought solutions on lines other than those of Western democracy.

The stage on which the drama of Irish history has been played took its shape through geological time, and it is littered with the human artefacts of 8,000 years. If historical discipline or human frailty makes us think of time as a series of acts or periods, we should always remember that the stage is never cleared for the next act and that man's choice of action at any point in time is restricted by actions previously taken. The importance and fascination of Ireland as a field for the study of land life and history lie in its small size, its insularity and in the unusual fact, so far as present evidence goes, that it was occupied by man so recently, in the time scale of human occupance of the earth, that investigations can begin with a *tabula rasa* and can trace, in theory, man's transformation of the pristine alongside changing technologies and societal forms through some eight millennia. It is an open air laboratory for the genetic study of man–nature relationships, and it was with this model in mind that a number of us at the Queen's University of Belfast have co-operated over the years in Irish field studies, including geomorphology, archaeology, palaeoecology, rural settlement, land-use and folklife. When we began, I found no apparent interest in these pedestrian pursuits among historians at Queen's, whose minds were on higher matters such as the British Constitution and Empire, and whose notable contributions to Irish historical studies were then hardly begun, but I found my first collaborator in a classical scholar, now living in South Africa, Professor Oliver Davies. History was to make amends. In due course, when the Faculty of Arts pressed for a School of Graduate Studies, it was Michael Roberts, Professor of Modern History, who championed the idea that it should not be confined to the humanities and should properly be concerned primarily with Ireland and all things Irish. In the end, the Institute of Irish Studies, of which I had the honour of being appointed the first Director (1965–70), was established with the pur-pose of 'stimulating and co-ordinating research in those subjects which have a particular Irish interest'. We have interpreted this in the widest terms, breaking away from the conventional restriction of Irish studies to literature, language and history.

In trying to sketch the personality of Ireland we may begin with the generalisation that most human societies, left to themselves, are conserving societies, and that cultural patterns, when they are adjusted to a particular environment – which is the price of their survival – tend to persist. For reasons which we considered in our second chapter, Ireland, despite its small area, is endowed with a variety of habitats, facilitating the survival of diverse groups in this insular end of the Old World. The primary food gatherers, at first confined to the flinty territory of the north-east coast and the fishy river Bann, found in time abundant opportunities elsewhere in inland rivers and lakes. Their characteristic artefacts are turning up further and further towards the west and south as archaeological fieldwork intensifies. It may well be that their last refuges were the peninsulas of Connemara and Kerry, where that Victorian pioneer observer of human types, John Beddoe, had picked out certain physical characteristics; for example, he notes that 'such a preponderance of dark hair does not, I believe, occur anywhere in Great Britain'.[9] And it has often been said that here there lingers the most magical charm of the Irish people. It would not surprise me if a strong Upper Palaeolithic strain persisted in the hardy fishermen and rock climbing fowlers who retained their food-gathering habits on some Atlantic coasts until recent times. I like to think that a Mesolithic heritage may explain, in part, the Irish fondness for lake islands, manifest in late Bronze Age lake dwellings, in early Celtic and medieval crannogs, in many a Christian monastery and in a long poetic tradition culminating in 'Innisfree'. And we may speculate on the roots of such marked Irish traits as an addiction to story-telling – for hunters and fishermen (and anglers) are notorious story-tellers – a fondness for moving melancholic folk music, often on an antique pentatonic scale, a wealth of international folk tales and a host of legends, highly imaginative stories and strange beliefs touching every native plant and animal. On analogy with the folkways of food-gathering societies surviving to this day in other parts of the world, these traits may have their roots deep in the Mesolithic substratum, however much they have been altered and added to. The use of heated stones for boiling meat in stone cists or wooden troughs, which smacks of ancient hunters and which can be traced back at least to the Bronze Age,[10] appears to have persisted to the end of the Middle Ages, and the popular name for the mounds of burnt stones which mark such camping sites (*fulachta fiadha* or deer roasts) suggests that an archaic tradition of hunting in roving bands was adopted by the Celtic aristocrats. The fact that the hunting season of the *Fiana* (the roving hunters and warriors hired by the Irish kings) lasted from May to November hints that this division of the year may be older than the pastoral rhythm of transhumance. More tangible but no less astonishing is the survival into our own day, in the very heart of the Pale, of a palaeotechnic artefact, the skin boat, represented by the

Boyne salmon-fishing curragh.[11] I have earlier referred to the heritage of aboriginal genes in a considerable proportion of the modern population, in Ulster as well as in the refuges of the western peninsulas. Those first Irishmen presumably came in from Scotland, but the typological evidence of their flint tools seems to point to cultural contact with the coasts of western Europe and of Scandinavia, the two ends of the Atlantic fringe of Europe in which Ireland occupies a central position. We recall the boastful words of an old Gaelic tract which refers to the early Christian centuries as a time when the world extended 'from Brittany to Norway and from the Orkneys to Spain'. Small wonder that the King of Spain's daughter and the Queen of Norway's son figure frequently in folk tales: the seas crossed by Viking longships and Spanish galleons had been navigated again and again in prehistory.

When we look at the Neolithic colonisation of Ireland, however, which would involve transport for families, livestock, fodder and seed corn, we must think of movements by land and of short sea passages.[12] The north-east was the first part to be settled, early in the fourth millennium, and indeed the nearest parallel to the ubiquitous leathery pottery of the north Irish Neolithic is to be found in the Yorkshire Wolds. The hunters and roving fishermen had already acquired a wide range of skills by 5000 B.C., and knew how to polish stone axes, and to these skills was now added the novelty of food production, particularly and understandably the herding of domesticated animals. We have referred to the far-reaching changes these innovations had on the landscape, and by the end of the fourth millennium farming communities were sufficiently stable to erect in the forest clearings elaborate stone monuments to serve as centres of burial and ritual. Anyone looking at the distribution of megaliths in Western Europe, where some 20,000 examples have survived into recent times, must be struck by their concentration in the islands and peninsulas of the Atlantic fringe from Portugal to Scandinavia. Ireland can show some 1,250 examples of such monuments, and they fall into several types. We have to explain both the distribution of the megaliths as a distinctive cultural phenomenon and their regional diversity. Theories as to their origins and their morphological evolution have had some strange and fanciful variants, but for many decades maritime diffusion from south-western Europe, whether by colonisers, traders, prospectors or missionaries, has been the generally accepted and most enlightened explanation; and a corollary of this hypothesis is that, in any receiving region such as Ireland, the oldest structures, being derived from a more advanced diffusing centre or from two or three such centres located somewhere between Malta and Brittany, should be the most elaborate and sophisticated examples, and simpler structures should be the product of regional devolution. I use the word 'enlightened' because one of the older explanations was associated with the concept of inevitable evolutionary progress and tainted by the exaggerated nationalism of the nineteenth century: it saw each country as a centre of independent development, and the megaliths in each region were accordingly classified in types which began with the simple and advanced to the complex. So long as absolute dates were not available, one could argue on typological grounds with much ingenuity for either theory – for devolution or for evolution. Various compromises between these views are now being advocated. Some startling dendrochronologically-adjusted C14 dates, for example a pre-4000 B.C. figure for some of the Breton passage graves, make a primary diffusion from Iberia extremely unlikely. A strong emotional current against diffusionism is now flowing. One idea that is gaining ground, however, is that certain megalithic forms were inspired by timber prototypes moving out of Central Europe by primary or secondary diffusion, that were given lithic form as they approached the stone-strewn landscapes of the Atlantic coasts and were adjusted to already existing faiths. (The classic example of a petrified timber monument of a later period is Stonehenge, where the lintels of the trilithons are secured by mortice and tenon joints.)

This is not the place to discuss the new theories, of which there are almost as many as there are investigators, but it is in line with the thesis of these lectures that what is emerging is a re-evaluation of the indigenous cultures of north-western Europe. Archaeology, dominated as it was, first by the historical model of successive more-or-less obliterating invasions and later by the diffusionism of the anthropologists, is now tending to confirm what recent anthropological linguistic and ethnographic research suggests, that the roots of regional personality in north-western Europe are to be found in the cultural experience of pioneer farmers and stockmen, quickened by the absorption of Mesolithic fisherfolk who were familiar with the Atlantic seas and who could have picked up ideas and techniques anywhere along the line. We must still reckon with a primary diffusion of crops and animals from the Near East, providing a more or less common base of material culture, while holding that the megalithic idea was expressed in different forms and different rituals from one region to another. It is significant that the earliest Irish megaliths, on present evidence, are the distinctive long court cairns of the north, in which there appears to be a strong element of the English long barrow and of timber antecedents. We know that blue-stone axes from County Antrim were being exported to many parts of Britain. It is a striking distributional fact that, of the 320 examples of court graves which have survived to be identified, less than half a dozen occur in the southern half of the island which is more accessible to diffusion from the mainland Atlantic coasts (fig. 5). One explanation that has been put forward, that they represent a colonising movement reaching Ireland through entries in remote County Mayo from an unspecified part of western France,[13] seems improbable on several grounds though one cannot deny multiple coastwise contacts. The passage graves with their round cairns and decorated stones, although more widely distributed throughout the country, are strongly concentrated in a few areas such as the Boyne valley, where they have an impressive size and splendour. The material elements of the Boyne culture, however, seem to be of native origin, and the pottery of the passage graves is profusely decorated with motifs made with the bone tools and netting cords appropriate to an acculturated Mesolithic population. It must be admitted that there is little archaeological trace of fisherfolk in the area, but a large labour force must have been available to the tomb builders, and there is the slender evidence of the Boyne curragh mentioned above. The Boyne salmon may indeed have played a central part in the conspicuous displays of the Boyne tombs, and their artistic exuberance, amounting to a *horror vacui*, may perhaps be reflected in the imaginative extravagances of early Celtic and early Christian art (pl. 2). The tombs find their closest parallels in Brittany but if there had been extensive colonisation from that direction we would expect to find more evidence of landings on the south coast, for which there is good evidence later on, for example, in the time of the wedge graves. All in all, it would seem that we should think of megalithic Ireland in terms of regions holding different religious beliefs. One might even see a puritanic earth-worshipping northern region, eschewing iconography, and a more artistic flamboyant sun-worshipping south, possessing much the same forms of material culture. Certainly, in the north of Ireland today differing religious faiths and rituals divide communities whose material ways of life are very similar. But I must resist the temptation to pursue this topic.

I am tempted to linger among the megaliths, however, for another reason, for it was while pursuing and excavating these astonishing witnesses to the faith and the technical skills of the farmers of 4,000 or 5,000 years ago that I became absorbed in the study of the peasant life that goes on around their ruins today. I felt that the land linked them together, and I was moved to look into the peasant heritage.[14] I had in mind the words of Fleure: 'The megaliths are not a matter of a vanished people and a forgotten civilization; they belong to the core of our heritage as western Europeans.'[15] But I also remembered the warning of Marc Bloch, that while the student of agrarian history misses much if he relies on documents alone, he must not leap at a bound from the eighteenth century to the Neolithic.[16] In Ireland, however, documentary or indeed any reliable data concerning peasant life is hard to find for periods before the seventeenth century, particularly for the Gaelic-speaking areas which then predominated. It has been estimated that about eighty per cent of modern historical writing on medieval Ireland is based on Norman and English sources. Scholars differ in the degree of reliance they place on the Gaelic records, the oldest of which were extensively revised and rewritten from the ninth century, and one has the impression that some enquirers have accepted what they wished to find and dismissed the rest as spurious. Even the Old Irish law tracts, which were apparently less Christianised – they were written down, Professor Binchy tells us, between the sixth and eighth centuries – and which clearly reflect the usages of a pagan age, give us only an abstract schematic picture of a highly stratified society and hardly touch the common people who must have constituted the mass of the population. How are we to make contact with them? I am comforted by the comment of Professor John Kelleher, that[17]

the culture that reasserted itself in the fourteenth century and continued viable . . . down to the early seventeenth century was but the latest stage of the culture that had existed continuously and strongly since prehistoric times . . . We can be sure that much of it survives in the native population, if only below the level of consciousness.

Contemporary studies, therefore, may throw light on a past of which history can tell us almost nothing. It is here that fieldwork – geographical, ethnological, anthropological, sociological – can contribute to our understanding. One can detect minor differences in the cultural landscapes of those parts of Ireland settled at various times by English or Scots – I am not referring to the landlords' demesnes which are singularly uniform in their landscaping but to the land worked on by former tenant farmers – but what is more significant is the extent to which, in fashioning it, the planters from Britain have taken over Irish habits. On a larger scale the example of India, or indeed of north America, reminds us that a diversity of human types and religions does not necessarily mean differences in material culture. I have referred to the rural house as an element in the cultural landscape which, despite regional variations, conforms to an Irish pattern. In Ulster, for example, the English planters soon gave up their half-timbered houses, partly no doubt because they could not stand up to the Irish predilection for incendiarism, and adopted native styles. Similarly agricultural implements, farming methods, domestic equipment, food, motor-habits, dialects and many customs and superstitions sooner or later took on an Irish flavour. The cultural absorption of the Anglo-Normans in most parts of their territory became proverbial. 'Lord how quickly doth that country alter one's nature', wrote the Elizabethan Spenser. The great seasonal festivals of the pastoral year were taken over and the gale days (rent days) are neither English nor Scottish but old Irish, May 1 and November 1, marking the beginning and the end of the summer grazing season when cattle were assembled and rents paid in kind. The territorial arrangements of the land are substantially unchanged despite improving landlords: the little townlands with their predominantly Gaelic names, the farm houses, small holdings and tiny towns, the intimate network of roads or boreens serving the scattered farms and relict clachans. Paradoxically it is much-planted Ulster that has the highest proportion of Gaelic place-names among the four provinces. In the west the scale of urban development hardly reaches medieval proportions. In a recent report on the Donegal Gaeltacht, the settlement of Falcarragh is referred to as 'one of the other larger towns'. Its population is given as 366. In Northern Ireland, the unconscious absorption of native ways is illustrated by the scorn with which the most extreme Bannside Unionist treats the Englishman who cannot get his tongue around such Gaelic place names as Ahoghill.

How does the personality of Ulster compare with that of Ireland as a whole? I see it as a strong regional variant, in habitat, heritage and history. Most of the nations of Europe have evolved through a fusion of regional loyalties, and their reconciliation calls for the exercise of tolerance and must always be subject to reservations. On economic grounds the term 'the Two Irelands' is often taken to refer to east and west rather than north and south, and in Cromwell's time it seemed that the Six Counties to be separated from the rest of Ireland were to be those of Connacht and Clare. In fact an east–west division, emphasised throughout the Middle Ages, is part of the nature of things. As in many other countries, however, the differences of outlook between north and south have been the most critical. The resultant tensions, for good and ill, are part of the island's personality. From the beginning, the north-east has been the easiest point of entry for newcomers whose leaders have tended increasingly, as communications have quickened, to maintain contacts with cross-channel homelands that are often within sight and rarely out of mind. Ulster has long had the reputation of breeding boastful and bellicose leaders mindful of their British origins and clinging to ideals and attitudes that the mother country was outgrowing. (The boastfulness may be partly explained as compensation for a colonial sense of inferiority.) It is significant that Ulster was able to supply a posse of anachronistic field marshals to serve the British army in the Second World War. It was the stubborn conservatism of pre-plantation Ulster that led, by delaying its conquest, both to the strength of its Gaelic heritage and to the scale and success of the seventeenth-century plantation. This was not only mainly and uncompromisingly Presbyterian but included a high proportion of farmers and artisans. Moreover, the influx was renewed in strength in the late seventeenth century, close contacts were maintained as industry expanded in the eighteenth, and, when communications were speeded up in the nineteenth, economic advantage was added to the attractions of political unionism.

The two communities in the north, however deeply divided by religion, share an outlook on life which is different from that prevailing in the south and which bears the stamp of a common heritage. They are alike in their intransigence. The epigrammatic concision of Ulster speech, most evident in the negative brevity of the notorious wall slogans, has been described as an essentially Gaelic quality.[18] Dialectal expressions are direct, earnest, decisive and often cynical. The traditional home industry of the north was based on the symbolically tough and long lasting flax fibre, and there was a strong radical element in the weavers. Both communities shared the benefits of what was known as the Ulster Custom, tenant right, and its bellicose spirit has outlived farm ownership, to the achievement of which it may be said to have pointed the way. It is idle to pretend that the differences between north and south are entirely the product of the Ulster plantation. If we take the longer view, we see them as a potential source of enrichment through cross-fertilisation, both in Ulster and in all Ireland. To achieve this, it seems to me, one should first look towards the renewal of regional consciousness in the old province of Ulster, and to a culturally productive borderland (p. 47).

The powerful grip of religious faith and practice has been one of the characteristic and divisive features of Irish life at many periods since the primary megalithic dichotomy. Because critical periods of external culture-contact appear to release energy and renew regional traditions, it is of particular interest to consider the early Christian centuries from this point of view. Ireland was the first non-Romanised part of Europe to be Christianised, and the new faith came face to face with archaic Celtic institutions and ancient pre-Celtic customs and beliefs. It was one of many periods when the western seaways of Europe were renewed, and Professor Bowen has pointed out parallels to megalithic diffusion;[19] and the parallels are all the closer if we abandon the idea of megalithic colonisation and think rather of contacts made during the seasonal activities of seafarers along the Atlantic coasts. Developing Mackinder's concept of positional geography, he has shown, by mapping the dedications of the Celtic churches, that groups of saints were active in different peninsular regions linked by sea, south-east Ireland being associated with south Wales, Cornwall and Brittany, for example, and north-east Ireland with south-west Scotland. It may be significant that early dedications to St Patrick appear to be most concentrated in the border drumlin belt and across the northern part of the Central Lowlands between two famous sites which bear his name, Downpatrick and Croagh Patrick. The supremacy of Armagh, the city of St Patrick, has been explained in many different ways, but one factor seems to have been the pagan prestige of nearby Navan and the spiritual capture of the critical border belt between north and south. Despite Patrick's triumph at Tara, his choice fell on Armagh. It seems that all was not harmony in the early centuries of Christianity and that, apart from the Palladian phase, an eremitical form of Christian practice was introduced into the south-east before St Patrick began his mission in the north. The apparent ready acceptance of Christianity, and its outstanding artistic achievements, surely reflect the recognition given to the professional classes of seers and craftsmen in the pagan Celtic world. And it is admitted, though piously understressed, that the early success of the Irish church was accompanied by the persuasion of supernatural happenings and by the popularity of miracle stories and legends of saints, many of whom bear the names and attributes of local deities. 'The Christian priests appear to have taken over the supernatural functions from the druids and *fili*.'[20] The pagan assemblies on sacred hilltops in early August, when the mid-point of the grazing season and the beginning of harvest were joyfully celebrated, may well have provided missionaries with receptive audiences, and it is interesting to notice that several 'patron heights' and many unblessed August gatherings on other hills crowned by prehistoric cairns, as well as the great Croagh Patrick pilgrimage, are located in the belt running from Mayo to Down. Such 'assemblies on hills' were among the native customs that the English strenuously opposed. The enduring success of Christianity in its conquest of Ireland was due to conscious and unconscious syncretism and its adjustment to the personality of Ireland: in fact it might be said with some truth that Ireland conquered Christianity. Here once more we see 'the power of the native tradition to assimilate new elements and to transmute them into something distinctively Irish'.[21] Finding no urban or legal base for a diocesan organisation, the Celtic church adopted the forms and framework of a scattered rural familial society. I cannot believe that the unparalleled popularity of the monastic life, as has been stated, was 'certainly an accident'.[22] It was not until the eighth century, however, that the privileged classes took over when the first missionary zeal had spent itself and the premature promise of Ireland as 'a sort of seventh-century Red China', in the words of Professor Kelleher,[23] faded away. The early church favoured a Mediterranean diet of bread and vegetables rather than whitemeats, and introduced new crops and techniques from the Roman world to encourage crop husbandry, but the pastoral life reasserted itself when the privileged native families gained monastic power, and before long, as Dr Lucas reminds us, powerful abbots were unashamedly demanding their tithe of the spoils of cattle-raids.[24] Such was the prestige of a church now gone native that the legendary histories of the country, as rewritten, amended and deliberately falsified by the clerics to enhance national prestige, to bolster princely privilege and to establish a respectable ancestry for the High Kingship of Tara,[25] were apparently accepted as broadly true by some scholars until half a century ago; and they have appeared in summary form in school text books down to our own day. Much of it was clearly learned nonsense and some scholars have expressed their admiration for methods of revision which Procrustes would have envied, but in so far as it was cast in the annalistic form of the Old Testament it was widely held in appropriate reverence. This dream world, moreover, offered consolation and compensation for the humiliating picture of the Irish presented by the standard English histories ever since the time of Giraldus Cambrensis. (Giraldus, it must be conceded, for all his prejudice, makes many observations that ring true. There is a grim topicality about his comment, made in the year 1185, that 'the Irish are quicker and more expert than any other people in flinging, when everything else fails, stones as missiles, and such stones do great damage to the enemy in an engagement'.)[26] Throughout the nineteenth century, a nationalist mythology, fed by a legitimate sense of grievance for past wrongs, which was endlessly reiterated in emotive phrases by Catholic racialist patriots such as O'Connell ('No people on earth were ever treated with such cruelty as the Irish') and by Presbyterian nationalists such as John Mitchel, with his vital vitriolic prose, was matched by the very different colonial mythology of the mass of the Protestant population; and these ancestral voices have not lost their vigour or their power to make trouble. Such patriotic sentiments have been artificially nurtured by home, school, church and press. In addition, Irish political history is complicated by repeated dissension among those who opposed the English. Mitchel's condemnation of the 'Carthaginians' was almost matched by his denunciation of O'Connell, the Old Irelander, 'next to the British Government, the worst enemy that Ireland ever had'.[27]

The insistence of the Catholic hierarchy on the sanctity of kin and family and the restrictions placed on marriage outside the faith, on contraception and divorce, have had many social political and demographic consequences, and have retarded the growth of communities based on loyalty to their common territories. (In theory, tribe and tribal territory (*túath*) were once synonymous.) Such pastoral patriarchal values have no doubt been sustained by recruitment to the service of the church from farming families and by the long association with conservative rural ways and traditions during penal days. It is said that, in some dioceses, the average age of clerics when they become priests is over sixty. It is interesting to note that the Irish word for family, *muinter*, is derived from *monasterium*. Father Ryan tells us that 'hatred of one's native district' was an axiom of monastic teaching.[28] Nurtured on an imaginative view of the past, it is apparently hard for many Irishmen to accept any other kind of history, or to see partition as anything more than a British imposition. The aim of the old clerical revisionists was not to seek truth or explain facts but to establish the fame of kings and high-kings. And because the basis was oral history, the Annals were cast in poetic or at least mnemonic form, using rhythm, alliteration and picturesque exaggeration as aids to the memory. The Anglo-Saxon is bewildered by this imaginative approach to what seems to him reality. It was an Irishman, admittedly from the drumlin belt, who wrote of his fellow countrymen: 'We tell the truth whenever a lie won't fit in.'[29] A literary approach to the past, while it must be one of the mainsprings of civilisation, has its dangers in a country which has a deep respect for intellectual values and for learning. The written word tends to carry conviction no matter how coloured by imagination or clouded by emotion. The acceptance of text as truth, however much distorted by evangelical oratory, has brought dangerous extremes of religious and political fundamentalism and intransigence. It is a tragedy that the common Irish heritage in material culture and folklife has been largely ignored until recently, not only in historical and political literature but in the entire educational system. I have been taken to task by clerics for talking of fireside furniture and spades instead of confining my attention to Celtic art when billed to lecture on old Irish handicrafts.

Here I may be permitted to pay tribute to my fellow geographers in Ireland, in school, college and university, for their insistence on the importance, whether in teaching or research, of direct field observation – a practice long familiar to naturalists – and for their pioneering work in local studies. It is a movement that began nearly half a century ago and is at last, I understand, being taken up by historians in some schools. Apart from its other benefits, first-hand knowledge of the visible heritage of cultural landscapes can be a powerful force in education for citizenship. It was the idea of a heritage shared by all sections of the community that inspired the movement leading to the passing of the Ulster Folk Museum Act (Northern Ireland) in 1958. The Folk Museum is intended to be an instrument of education and research as well as a demonstration of traditional crafts and values, and its success in these difficult times is a most promising sign. I would recall also the work done by a group of devoted scholars in the nineteenth century, when the Ordnance Survey Memoirs were designed to accompany and illuminate the first accurate maps of Ireland. The plan was conceived by Colonel Thomas Colby, Director of the Surveys of England and Ireland, but it was Thomas Larcom who developed it in 1832 and enrolled the assistance of scholars such as John O'Donovan and Eugene O'Curry working under the general supervision of George Petrie.[30] Larcom planned the work of the *Historical Commission* in three parts, using much the same three-pronged approach as I am advocating. 'Geography', he wrote, 'is a noble and practical science only when associated with history.' He saw the 'social and productive economy' of the country in all its variations as the product of two forces, 'the state of nature and the state of man'. The Memoirs were intended 'to hold up the past as a beacon and a guide to the future',[31] and if they had been completed as planned they would have given us an invaluable cross-section of early Victorian Ireland. Those Memoirs which were completed as originally intended are indeed of great value – the manuscripts are in the library of the Royal Irish Academy – but after the first volume was published the Commission was cut back by Lord Melbourne in 1839, 'in a fit of ill-timed parsimony': in reality, one suspects, because their revelations of the strength of the Irish heritage and the condition of the peasantry did no credit in his eyes to several centuries of British rule. This was not the first time that Ireland had served as a model for trying out new cartographical techniques and associated surveys. In the seventeenth century it became the testing-ground for the theories of Sir William Petty, a man of remarkable versatility, whom Karl Marx referred to as the father of modern political economy.[32] Petty was also a geographer in that he insisted that environmental conditions provided a clue to the human condition and that the map should be the link between the land and humane studies. Larcom seems to have drawn inspiration from Petty; and a French writer, Yan Goblet, called Petty the spiritual father of Vidal de la Blache.

I propose to select for brief comment one of the many subjects which the material in the Ordnance Survey Memoirs illuminates, namely transhumance or booleying. If documentation of agrarian history is thin, it is almost entirely lacking when we come to consider its content of nomadism. Field observation and oral tradition, however, have provided evidence of the former practice of seasonal nomadism in nearly every hill region where it has been sought. The booleying life, from its nature, leaves little in the way of artefacts for the archaeologist to discover and date, but on analogy with other transhumant societies in the mountainous parts of Europe, it may be another prehistoric culture element. As we know it from recent survivals and from folk memory, booleying was essentially a custom of lowly folk, but this was not always so. In other lands of transhumance, the practice has long been an integral part of the total economy and there is no reason to suppose that Ireland was an exception despite the scant reference to the custom in the early literature. From about the year 1700, however, we have a description of the 'booley or summer habitation' of O'Flaherty, the chief of a Connacht clan, which was situated some miles away from his winter home. It was a long house of hurdles, thatched, and it was rebuilt every year. In addition to his flocks and herds he kept 'nine brace of wolf dogs, as ornaments and for hunting deer'.[33] The deer, it should be noticed, also sought the high pastures in summer, and ancient hunters following them would readily have taken to transhumance. There is a possibility, however, that seasonal movement may originally have taken the form of 'inverse transhumance', from occupation sites among the hills to the lowland forests in summer. Braudel regards this downhill movement from the occupied hills as the older form of transhumance in the Mediterranean region, and M. Louis considers that the megaliths of Languedoc were built by pastoral transhumants. A similar association is suggested for the limestone plateau of the Burren in County Clare, famed for its 'winterage' as well as for its wedge graves.

Today, cattle are taken to the Burren for winter grazing and are said to thrive on it.[34]

The nakedness of the Irish hills, where the original forest cover is reduced to a thin scatter of thorny bushes, must have been accelerated by extensive common grazing in summer. We get the impression from folk tradition that, where booleying was practised, life began and ended with the herding of cattle, and the Irish word for a boy, *buchail,* means a herder. Great numbers of the migrant harvesters of last century who paved the way for permanent migrants to Great Britain came from north-western Ireland, where booleying long persisted. I have elsewhere referred to this movement as an extended transhumance, and I have since discovered that in Donegal the migratory season of the spalpeens ran from May 1 to November 1, which were the traditional dates for movement to and from the summer pastures (see Appendix). The summer months were similarly the favourite season for foot-free 'travelling men' of all kinds, and for coastwise trading. The once thriving coastal shipping trade of another pastoral region, Cardiganshire, which operated during the six summer months, has been described as a maritime transhumance – a transmerance. We are reminded of the two mighty voices of Wordsworth, of the freedom offered by hills and the sea. Land-bound peasants lacking these opportunities and firmly attached to the soil and to crop husbandry will be more ready to accept a conqueror than cattlefolk accustomed to some form of pastoral nomadism whose first loyalties are to kin and kine and who are prepared to move rather than submit. During the seventeenth century plantations of Ulster, dispossessed natives were able to survive by taking to the hills and adopting for a time a completely nomadic life. These lawless rovers were known as creaghts, an anglicised form of *creach* (a herd of cattle, and in earlier times a cattle raid) and the word 'creaght' came to be applied also, apparently by confusion with *creat* (crate), to the hurdle-framed houses which they moved from one pasture to another and which, like the more permanent houses of mud or stone which have survived, were covered with long turves.[35]

Another topic on which the Memoirs throw much light is that of field fences, whether ancient examples often referred to as 'Danes' fences' or more recent types of stone walls or sod or clay banks. Nothing is more characteristic of the Irish lowlands than small fields and tall hawthorn hedges, more typical of the hill slopes than untidy stone walls. The so-called Celtic field system of tiny fields enclosed by fences of stone earth or sods has also characterised much of Scotland and Highland Britain as well as Brittany: the dyke of Scotland, the clawdd of Wales, the talus of Brittany, the ditch of Ireland. For the Englishman the word 'ditch' calls for explanation since to him it signifies a depression. It is said that one of Sir James Craig's speeches in the British House of Commons, made during a debate on fox-hunting, caused much bewilderment because of its Irishness. Irish horses, he said, were not troubled by difficult fences because they could change feet on top of the ditch, and his listeners were left with a charming picture of equine ballet-dancers. The English field hedge, well trimmed and graced by great hedgerow trees, was planted at ground level, whereas the Irish hedge is grown in a bank. Along the Atlantic fringe, the drystone wall is a cultural form as old as the first farmers, and its origins may be partly explained by the field clearance of large stones in rock-strewn or glaciated environments. In early Christian and medieval times, farmsteads and monasteries alike were enclosed by massive walls or banks, partly no doubt as a defence against cattle thieves. When wolves or other predators were no longer a serious threat, farmsteads and adjacent small fields or 'gardens' were still enclosed by lesser banks, bitten bare except for prickly shrubs but topped as required with dead thorns. 'Naked fences with a crest of blackthorn' are mentioned in Old Irish laws dating from the eighth century. When the practice of using live thorns was introduced, possibly in the sixteenth century, they were planted in the banks, producing the untidy hedges and poor hedgerow timber that disgusted English visitors such as Arthur Young. The well-enclosed lowland landscapes, as we know them, took shape mostly under agrarian change between 1750 and 1850, and the landlords who fashioned them adopted and improved the indigenous system of banked enclosures to the making of which the native spades and shovels were adapted. Some landlords, in order to give hedgerow trees a better footing, built wide double ditches consisting of a large central bank planted with trees and a hedged bank on each side. The regional variations of styles of ditches and spades are of great geographical interest. Let me add that the distributional studies of landlordism, tenure, landscape and land-use made by a geographer, Professor Jones Hughes, have a close bearing on topics such as agrarian unrest which are the historian's concern.

Cattlemen throughout the ages have had little use for urban centres save as places where fairs are held. They have been more willing to raid and ruin architectural works than to build them and it has been observed that the Irish have a genius for turning towns built by others into slums. Sheer poverty, however brought about, has been a contributing factor, and many urban immigrants in the nineteenth century came from lonely cabins and clachans, bringing with them unhygienic habits and a toleration for crowded kinsfolk which depressed the standards of urban living. But still, in round figures, taking Ireland as a whole, about half the population of four-and-a-half million lives outside towns of any size. For most farmers, livestock, and especially cattle, are a dominant interest. For Irish people 'meat' means beef, and the consumption per head of milk and milk products is about the highest in the world, despite a general disregard for cheese. Livestock and livestock products have been prominent in exports since medieval times, and today they make the largest single contribution to the total economy of the country.

The whole nature of Gaelic society was opposed to urban living, and where this society lasted longest, notably in Ulster, towns and townscapes are almost without exception post-medieval. Yet much of Celtic Europe was already proto-urban in the last centuries B.C., and before long the expansion of Rome brought the urban forms and institutions of the Mediterranean world to Western Europe, but not to Ireland. One may speculate on what a Roman occupation, or indeed an Anglo-Saxon colonisation which it also missed, might have done for the island, but their absence certainly favoured continuity. Not until early Christian times did it receive a thin scatter of monastic proto-towns which, although of considerable size, lacked the trading functions of true towns. Even the hill forts of the late Bronze and early Iron Ages, which one looks for as the Dublin Castles of the Celtic kings, are few in number and strange in form. The most famous examples such as Tara, Navan and Dun Aillinne are simple and usually circular enclosures, doubtfully defensive but providing protection rather against the spirit world, for the surrounding fosse lies not outside but inside the rampart, as in the older henge monuments. The town in Ireland is the mark of the invader, and Professor Quinn has shown that Elizabethan colonisers, using Ireland as a testing ground for trans-Atlantic ventures, saw towns as symbols of law, peace and civilisation in savage lands, and themselves as 'colonels' after the Roman model.[36] In Gaelic Ireland, towns have remained small. In 1841, when the population was approaching its maximum of about 8,500,000, nearly twice its present size, only fifteen per cent lived in towns, most of them very small, while by that time nearly half the population of Britain was urban, Dublin alone reaching a quarter of a million. Belfast, however, was growing rapidly, and a century later, in 1941, the two capitals were not very different in size. The partition of Ireland which gave political recognition to this duality had come about twenty years earlier, but the concept of two nations had been in the air since the early nineteenth century. Professor Max Heslinga traces Ulster nationalism back to the seventeenth century plantation of Scots Presbyterians, but if one thinks in terms of regionalism the division is far older. He regards the land boundary between Ulster and the Republic as an extension of the historic border between Scotland and England[37] but to argue, as he does, that the close social and economic ties between England and the Republic make the Irish Sea less of a cultural divide than the Ulster border is to overlook the essential unity of Ireland in terms of personality and to overestimate the significance of Dublin in Irish life. The urban – rural continuum which makes England uniquely megalopolitan does not extend far beyond metropolitan Dublin and the few sizeable towns. Despite political pressures, economic considerations for the bulk of the Irish people have not so far openly outweighed spiritual values. The Irish Sea remains a religious divide, and in the absence of linguistic identity, despite the official position given to the Gaelic language, religion has played a larger part in the symbolism of the state.

I have stressed the striking continuities of culture and landscape as factors with which political and economic historians have not concerned themselves but which, in my view, throw a revealing light on the character of Ireland. We have to consider how these continuities can be reconciled with genetic change and with evolving external arrangements in the organisation of political life. On the first point, the example of the Aran Islands demonstrates what we believe to be generally true, that cultural continuity does not imply genetic continuity. On the second point, we have seen that institutional change, whether brought about by primary or secondary diffusion, has been achieved within an older framework of local and regional units by an enlargement of authority. Dissident elements in the past, their mobility facilitated by nomadic or pastoral habits, have been able to take refuge in the hills or among the bogs, or at times to move overseas, go underground, or be attracted into the new hierarchy. Politically and culturally, successive newcomers have been able to achieve no more than a half conquest, and much of the character of Ireland springs from the tensions thus engendered. The brilliant achievements of Anglo-Irish literature can be paralleled in many earlier cultural blossomings in which one may detect the inspiration of contact with indigenous cultures. Instead of being replaced these are reborn under the impact of new cultures. In our own day, a rich vein of oral tradition has revitalised creative writing. The very poverty of the tattered ends of Europe has helped to preserve old values, to favour personal expression in poetry, oratory, music and song, where one man is as good as the next and all are independent of capital equipment, rather than in those arts requiring joint endeavour and a large investment. The unlettered countryman often displays remarkable powers of memory and takes delight in a language that differs in many ways from standard English. Thanks to such continuities, Ireland has more than once been able to hand back to the outside world gifts which it received and enriched with its own genius.

It has been my contention in these lectures that historical studies would be enriched if they paid more attention to habitat and heritage and that closer co-operation with geography and anthropology would be fruitful. In the dedicated scholarship of both Anglo-Irish and Celtic historians, one sees little attention given to these matters. Conventional history is at a loss where, as in the west of Ireland, history and prehistory seem to co-exist and all time is fore-shortened into a living present. To the specialist in the history of restricted periods it may well appear that the most powerful forces of history are individual personality and free-will.

On the longer view, I believe that the personality of society as a whole is a powerful motive force and that it finds expression in the cultural landscape. While it is becoming fashionable to show an interest in the human environment, even among politicians, I do not expect to have convinced the literary addict that the physical environment as fashioned by man is worthy of his attention, or that the land itself is something more than a picturesque stage for cultural achievement, but I find support for my view in the perceptive regionalism of many creative writers. Geographers are not alone in stressing the significance of habitat and heritage in the shaping of the human experience. True, we might well be spared the facile couplings of Irish mist and Celtic mystery, of black basalts and black Presbyterians, creameries and dreameries, or indeed, you may add, of poverty and poetry, drums and drumlins. We may have our doubts about Filson Young's statistical correlations of pastoralism, paternalism and puritanism with mental deterioration and lunacy, and about his conclusion: 'better a hundred bastards than one lunatic!'[38] And yet: I have in mind writers such as D.H. Lawrence, Norman Douglas and Lawrence Durrell. 'We tend to see culture', writes Durrell, 'as a sort of historic pattern dictated by the human will . . . but the ambience and mood, the manners and habits of a people exist in nature, as a function of place.' He sees 'an enduring faculty of self expression inhering in a landscape' and concludes that 'the important determinant of any culture is the spirit of place'.[39] And the musicologist, Alan Lomax, claiming that regional personality is reflected in musical styles, language forms and associated reasoning processes, in gestures and other body movements, has gone some way to prove his point by an impressive array of distribution maps, photographs and films.[40]

The scientist, in trying to explore the roots and measure the strength of regional personality, should welcome the support that comes from the intuitive understanding and interpretation of the creative writer, the poet, the music-maker and the artist, even if they cannot be quantified. Their inspiration characteristically springs from intimate association with particular landscapes, local, regional or national. Similarly, true patriotism grows out of attachments to small territories within the compass of youth's consciousness. And when it comes to writing agrarian history – I quote Marc Bloch once more – 'it is only on the small scale where interpretation can be checked against observation and local knowledge that definitive conclusions can be reached'. I may add that my own understanding of rural Ireland, such as it is, was enriched by a study, made many years ago, of a small *túath* which keeps its old title in popular speech – the Kingdom of Mourne.

Facts from Gweedore

Gweedore (fig. 10) is a district in the Donegal Gaeltacht to the south of the Bloody Foreland in the extreme north-west of Ireland. It is secluded in a wasteland of blanket bog beyond the bold quartzite cone of Errigal. Two outstanding figures are associated with it in the history and folk memory of the nineteenth century – Lord George Hill the landlord and Father James McFadden the patriot priest – but the interest of Gweedore extends far beyond personalities and agrarian disputes: for the cultural geographer and the anthropologist it is a model of a region of difficulty and survival. Lord George Hill is best known through his pamphlet *Facts from Gweedore*, with its graphic accounts of rural poverty and of the working and dissolution of the rundale system and the associated practice of booleying. Recently it was reprinted by the Institute of Irish Studies, Queen's University, Belfast, and what follows is a slightly condensed version of the present writer's introduction to the reprint together with some extracts from the work itself. *Facts from Gweedore* is also a revealing exposure of an apparently irresolvable clash of cultures. Indeed it would be difficult to find two personalities more representative of Englishry and Irishry than Hill and McFadden. The techniques of resistance to authority and 'reform', the withholding of rents, the appeals for American support, the stone-throwing and other acts of violence, the war of words, the two views of Ireland and the differing interpretations of truth: all this, transferred to an urban setting, is with us in Ulster today.

Lord George Hill's pamphlet, which describes the appalling agrarian condition of Gweedore in the years immediately preceding the Great Famine and his efforts to ameliorate it, was widely read at the time and attracted the attention – and the financial contributions – of many philanthropic bodies. It also called forth rejoinders from many Irish writers who saw the author's attempts to improve the lot of the peasants, which they called 'improving them off the land', as yet another example of a landlord's greed. But apart from the part it played in the bitter controversy over Irish landlordism, the pamphlet has long been valued for its factual account of the system of land-use known in Ireland as rundale, akin to the better-known runrig system of Scotland. Despite all the attempts to eradicate it, rundale has survived here and there in north-west Donegal, in a reduced and modified form, into our own time, and it was in Gweedore that the present writer discovered and described these survivals over thirty years ago. *Facts from Gweedore* was first published in 1845, and

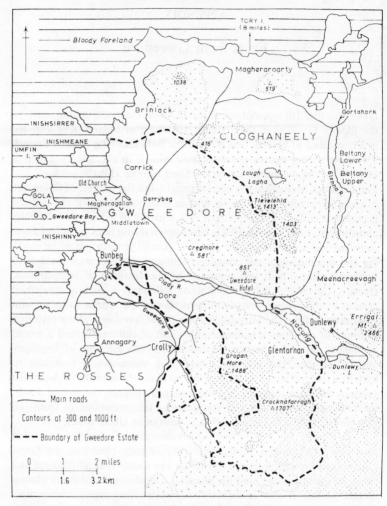

Fig. 10. The Gweedore district.

a note attached to the fifth and last edition (1887) states: 'It was strange that that particular property should have been singled out for a playground for politicians.' Yet 'this simple record of a good man's work' must have been partly responsible because of the publicity it received. Gweedore became indeed not only a playground but at times a battleground.

For all its self-righteousness the pamphlet was a genuine attempt to arouse interest in the plight of the Irish peasantry. Yet calumnies were heaped upon its author, as one of 'the rackrenting horde of land speculators', and it was rumoured that it was he who had betrayed Wolfe Tone at Lough Swilly in 1798, although he was not then born: the real culprit was Sir George Hill. Many stories about Lord George are current in Gweedore, some vilifying him as a tyrant and an evictor, others paying tribute to his kindness and his knowledge of the Irish language. The written accounts are similarly contradictory. The authoress of *John Halifax, Gentleman*, visiting Gweedore in 1886, writes: 'Of Lord George Hill I have heard two diametrically opposed accounts, each vouched for with equal violence.'[1] A note in the fourth edition of the pamphlet tells us that Lord George 'expended upon the Gweedore property, during the first 14 years, all the rents received from the tenants, besides large sums derived from other sources', but Denis Holland, a Belfast journalist with strong nationalist sympathies (proprietor and editor of the *Ulsterman*), wrote that he not only 'never expended a shilling in improving the lands on which his tenants dwell', but that he spent the funds that poured in for famine relief 'in building pretty roads through his own exclusive lands and making the fancy hotel more approachable'.[2] The pamphlet was described as 'the cheapest engine by which any man ever won a good name'. In the eyes of Stephen Gwynn, Hill was 'a very pattern of gentleness and courtesy' . . . 'no man has done so much to redeem the reproach that rests on Irish landlordism'.[3] But Holland satirises him as 'a special blessing on two legs, sent by Providence for the comfort of the neglected Celts of the wilds of Donegal' and describes Gweedore as 'the region where Irish landlordism is most sordid, cruel and rapacious'. Another opinion comes from a celebrated visitor 'from the severity of whose awful pen not many people escaped'. Thomas Carlyle met Hill in 1849, having been driven from Kilmacrenan along 'a bleak dismal 22 miles of road' to the Gweedore Hotel. Lord George lived at Ballyarr near Kilmacrenan, and Carlyle observes: 'this is the road he drives every week these 17 years.' Carlyle describes him as 'a man you love at first sight, handsome, gravely smiling; thick grizzled hair, military composure' (he had retired from the British army with the rank of major), and he extols his efforts: 'It is the largest attempt at benevolence and beneficence on the *modern* system ever seen by me or like to be seen.' But Carlyle saw also the inevitable clash of two cultures: 'Alas, how can it prosper, except to the soul of the noble man himself who earnestly tries it and works at it, making himself a slave to it these 17 years.' 'In all Ireland' he concludes, 'saw no such beautiful soul.'[4]

Lord George Augustus Hill (1801–79) was the fifth and posthumous son of the second Marquis of Downshire, a descendant of the planter Moyses Hill who settled in County Down in 1573 and whose family name is commemorated in that county in such place names as Hill Hall, Hillsborough and Hilltown. Receiving no legacy, it seems that his family provided him with sufficient capital to leave Hillsborough and to purchase, from 1838 onwards, some 23,000 acres of land in the parish of Tullaghobegly West, in the barony of Kilmacrenan, extending northwards along the coast from the Gweedore River. Hill stated that he first saw the district when touring the west coast in 1834. The property included several offshore islands, the largest of which was Gola. Although the *Parliamentary Gazetter* of 1844 briefly dismisses Gweedore as 'the name of a rivulet, a bay and a wretched fishing hamlet', the name is now applied to an extensive district lying between Cloghaneely to the north-east and the Rosses to the south-west. It is also the name of a Roman Catholic parish established in the 1830s, and it was the name given by Lord George to his hotel, built by the Clady River in 1842, to which was attached a model farm which had about twenty acres of arable land. The hotel was closed in 1945, and the hotel and farm buildings are now unoccupied and at the mercy of vandals, although they still contain some relics of the Hill period. Another melancholy reminder of a vanished age is Gweedore Station, situated near the hotel on a branch of the Londonderry and Lough Swilly Railway which operated from Letterkenny to Burtonport from 1903 until 1940.

Nineteenth-century visitors describe the area as one of desolate savagery, and even today, once one leaves the densely-settled coast road, it is singularly wild and empty, consisting mostly of blanket bog. Much of the cultivated land is reclaimed from peat and boulders, and along the coast rock exposures alternate with sand dunes. Inland it culminates in the naked hill mass of Tievelehid (1413 feet). Granite underlies most of the area, and the higher hills are composed of resistant quartzite, but patches of schist occur in some of the river valleys, and thin bands of ancient limestone bring relative fertility to parts of the Clady valley. Like most of Donegal it was classified as a congested district in 1891, and today it is near the heart of the Donegal Gaeltacht. Settlement clings to the lowlands below about 250 feet, and the whole coastal strip from the Bloody Foreland to the Gweebarra River is thickly settled, with population densities probably exceeding 300 people per square mile of cultivated land: in 1891 the figure reached 400.[5] There were no roads fit for wheeled vehicles until 1834, when the Board of Works completed the road to the Gweedore River from Dunlewy: the bridge was built in 1840. The evidence suggests that communications in former times were mainly by sea. Lord George records almost incredible feats of seamanship with the Bunbeg curragh, a wicker vessel measuring only nine feet by three, 'skinned' with tarred canvas, (formerly with a hide), which is of unusual interest in being one of the few surviving sea-going paddle-curraghs (see tailpisce). He writes:

Another instance of the rash and reckless daring of these islanders may be told – it happened recently and in the neighbourhood. A man and his wife coming out of the Island of Arranmore, in a little boat filled with turf, had a horse standing on the top of it; with the roll of a sea, the animal was thrown out, and as they were a long way from land, must have been drowned, had not the man cleverly succeeded in getting him into the boat again!

Since prehistoric times the population of west Donegal has clung to the coast: megalithic monuments – abundant in south-west Donegal – are nearly all near the sea, and in the Rosses there are traces of sand-dune settlements, some of them dating from the Bronze and Early Iron Ages. This coastal concentration of population is characteristic of much of western Ireland, but it is doubtful if there was much permanent settlement in Gweedore until recent centuries. There are a few early Christian sites in the area, including the remains of a medieval church on the *machair* at Magheragallan, but it seems likely that intensive settlement began with refugee movements from the east associated with the Ulster plantations of the seventeenth century.[6]

In Gweedore, hard-won cultivated 'infields' on the narrow strip of lowland between the hills and the *machair* provided a base whose meagre resources could be supplemented on the one hand by the extensive mountain grazing stretching inland and on the other by various sea products – fish and shellfish, as well as sea-weed used for manuring and kelp burning and for providing relish or 'kitchen' for a potato diet. One of the most interesting passages in *Facts from Gweedore* relates to a complex form of transhumance, a subject of great interest to the cultural geographer.

It often happens that a man has three dwellings – one in the mountains, another upon the shore, and the third upon an island, he and his family flitting from one to another of these habitations as the various and peculiar herbage of each is thought to be beneficial to the cattle, which are supposed, at times, to have a disease requiring change of pasture, whilst in reality they only want more food. This change usually takes place upon a fixed day, the junior branches of the family generally perform the land journey on the top of the household goods, with which the pony may often be seen so loaded, and at the same time so obscured, that little more than the head can be observed; and thus the chair or two, the creels, and the iron pot, the piggin, and the various selected *et cetera* – as if invested with a sort of dull locomotive power – creep along the roads. The little churn is slung on the side of the animal, into which the youngest child is often thrust, its head being the only part visible; and in this plight it resembles, in various particulars, a sweep peeping and screeching too, at the top of a chimney.

The shore dwellings, clustered together in 'clachans' on the edge of the infields, were the main base. Most of the livestock would be driven to the mountain grazing for the summer, when the infields were under crops, and it was mainly in the autumn, according to one account, that they were taken to the islands, where there had apparently been little permanent settlement until the eighteenth century. It seems probable that on the islands, as in many of the townlands on the slopes of Tievelehid, the booleys were replaced by permanent habitations as population increased and old habits weakened. Here as in other parts of Ireland the mountain pastures were named after the townland which claimed the right to use them, and some of them were later given the status of separate townlands, e.g. Magheraroarty Mountain, Beltany Mountain. The *machair* was utilised in early summer. Dr Desmond McCourt tells me that down to about 1940 young folk from adjacent townlands would bring cattle and spend a few weeks tending them in the *machair* of Magheragallan, where some of the abandoned byre-houses may still be seen. Old people recall that it was a time of much merriment, and they look back with nostalgia to the freedom of the booleys. Such nomadic habits – the ease with which cattle could be taken to the safety of the mountains – help to explain the effective resistance of the area to landlordism until the early nineteenth century, and the strength of the opposition to Lord George's improvements. The diminutive size of these seasonal dwellings, moreover, seems to have set a restricting pattern for the more permanent houses which succeeded them.

In many parts of western Ireland it has been remittances from overseas migrants that have helped to maintain a dense population, but particularly in north-west Donegal the main factor was the money earned by the seasonal migrants who went in summer on farm work to Scotland but also to the protestant areas in east Donegal. Some parts of north-west Donegal actually showed an increase of population in the decades following the Famine, when the rural population in Ireland generally fell drastically. At the end of the last century, when eighty-seven per cent of the holdings had a rateable value of less than £2, it was estimated that nearly forty per cent of the entire population of Gweedore were migrant seasonal labourers.[7] Home industries such as weaving and knitting which Lord George did much to encourage have long been another source of income (Hill patriotically boasts that 'during the Crimean war we furnished the South Down Militia with a great proportion of their socks') and they now supply a lively tourist market. Increasingly, permanent or semi-permanent emigration has taken the place of seasonal movement. The spalpeens are now few in number and the summer season sees instead an in-movement of holiday-makers: though the district lost fifteen per cent of its permanent population between 1951 and 1961 through emigration, the coast road has become a thriving but uncontrolled and untidy ribbon of settlement.

Before 1838 there were no resident landlords in Gweedore and apparently no land-agents. There were a great many absentee proprietors, some of them claiming only a single townland, with a nominal rent of a few pounds. The average annual rent of the holdings, some 700 in number, was 14s; and if rent was paid at all it was collected at livestock fairs or settled in poteen. Many of the holdings had half 'a cow's grass', or less, of arable land – a cow's grass amounting to about three acres.[8] The arrears of rent were estimated at £1000. The countryside was virtually unenclosed save for the sod or stone fences marking the townland boundaries, and even yards or gardens were almost unknown. The land was treeless and hard-bitten by grazing stock which were allowed to wander freely, in summer in the mountain commonage, in winter through each townland. Under the rundale system a number of tenants, up to twenty or more, held the arable land jointly, each family's plots, separated only by untilled balks, being scattered through the open 'infield'; and they had rights of turbary, of outfield cultivation, mountain grazing and seaweed gathering in proportion to their arable holdings. The arable infield might comprise most of a small townland of say 200 acres or it might be confined, in large townlands stretching up into the mountains, to a restricted area of relatively good land. Cultivation, of oats and potatoes, was entirely by spade. There were no hay meadows and no rotation grasses.

The houses were loosely grouped in 'towns' or 'villages' for which the Scottish term 'clachan' was used in some parts of Ulster; and this word, which I proposed as a generic term when I first described such Donegal house-clusters – to distinguish them from the more complex 'villages' of the English openfield system – has been widely adopted for rural settlements of this type, associated with the rundale openfield system. They were 'farm-towns', without church or chapel, shops or public houses. These clusters in some parts of Donegal were already at the beginning of the century 'dispersing daily into separate habitations and holdings'[9] as the rundale system fell into decay, and even in the north-west some re-distribution had taken place before 1834. Much of the Rosses, to judge from the Ordnance Survey maps, had dispersed dwellings at that time, and in Gweedore there were already some isolated houses, probably associated with land reclamation. In general, though there were some discrete clusters, the pattern of settlement in Gweedore was one where the houses were strung together along hillside tracks, gathering here and there into knots. New houses were being added to the clusters as holdings were subdivided. The occupants were inter-related kin-groups, held together by the ties of kinship and of mutual help and protection. In earlier times it seems that the infield plots were periodically redistributed by lot-casting, and since no one knew where his plots might be located it was anyhow most convenient for the houses to be grouped together. As Lord George describes the system, the plots had been repeatedly subdivided among co-heirs until they were sometimes reduced to a few square yards, and he gives an instance where a horse was shared by three men, each claiming one leg, with the result that the fourth leg remained unshod.

The wretched system of Rundale being here in full force and operation, all this district of country is held under what is known by that term, and which may be thus described: In some instances, a tenant having any part of a townland (no matter how small), had his *proportion* in thirty or forty different places, and without fences between them, it being utterly impossible to have any, as the proportions were so very numerous, and frequently so small, that not more than half a stone of oats was required to sow one of such divisions. Thus every tenant considers himself entitled to a portion of each various quality of land in his townland; and the man who had some good land at one extremity, was sure to have some bad at the other, and a bit of middling in the centre, and bits of other quality in odd corners, each bounded by his neighbour's property, and without any fence or ditch between them. Under such circumstances as these, could any one wonder at the desperation of a poor man, who having his inheritance in *thirty-two* different places, abandoned them in utter despair of ever being able *to make them out!*

Fights, trespasses, confusion, disputes and assaults, were the natural and unavoidable consequences of this system; these evils, in their various forms, were endless, and caused great loss of time and expense to the people attending petty sessions; and, of course, continued disunion amongst neighbours, was perpetuated. The system, too, was a complete bar to any attempt at improvement; as, on a certain day, all the cattle belonging to the townland were brought from the mountains and allowed to run indiscriminately over the arable land, and any that had not their potatoes dug, or other crops off the ground, were much injured; neither could any one man venture to grow turnips, clover, or other green crops, for nothing short of a seven feet wall would keep out the mountain sheep. To add to this, no one would attempt to manure better, or otherwise improve his proportion, as his neighbour's cattle only would have the benefit; and in spring no individual occupier of the division, would set or sow, or labour in the fields, before a certain day, when the cattle were again sent to the hills, until after harvest.

By the time of the Great Famine, although rundale persisted in many parts of western Ireland, the system was breaking down and was losing its purpose as a market economy, and new means of communication were affecting the old subsistence life. A good deal of evidence on the subject can be gleaned from the Minutes of Evidence of the Devon Commission (1845–7) but by that time rundale was in decline. We look in vain for any descriptions of this important cultural phenomenon among the copious outpourings of nineteenth-century nationalist writers who were full of praise for the good old days, when the people 'used and enjoyed the land without let or hindrance'.[10] It is ironic that *Facts from Gweedore*, which contains one of the fullest accounts we have of this indigenous Irish practice, should come from one who was committed to its destruction.

The new landlord immediately set about abolishing the rundale system and breaking up the house clusters. Objections of all kinds were raised by the tenants, but the greatest objection seems to have been taken to the house-scattering. There were complaints about 'the solitary grandeur of the new dwellings' though they were neither solitary nor grand. Even on the new squared farms they were rarely more than 100 or 200 yards apart, and on the narrowest strip farms they were separated by no more than a few yards. Most of the houses in the clusters seem to have been one-roomed hovels. Indeed, throughout the west of Ireland, down to late in the nineteenth century, 'the majority of the inhabitants were housed in one-roomed hovels, built of sods or mud, without windows or chimneys'.[11] Nevertheless most of the houses in the Gweedore clusters appear to have been stone-built, perhaps because refugees brought with them a tradition of building in stone. They were, however, utterly comfortless. Although some of the houses had a built-in bed, placed in a projecting wing in a side-wall (the 'outshot') most of the family slept on straw, rushes or heather spread on the floor in front of the fire, and 'all in the bare buff', according to Patrick McKye, whose memorial, contained in *Facts from Gweedore*, is as follows. (McKye was the teacher in the National School, and the memorial is dated 1837. The population of the parish, as given in 1841, was not 4000 but about 9000.)

To His Excellency the Lord Lieutenant of Ireland.
THE MEMORIAL OF PATRICK M'KYE.

MOST HUMBLY SHEWETH,

That the parishioners of this parish of West Tullaghobegly, in the Barony of Kilmacrennan, and County of Donegal, are in the most needy, hungry, and naked condition of any people that ever came within the precincts of my knowledge, although I have travelled a part of nine Counties in Ireland, also a part of England and Scotland, together with a part of British America. I have likewise perambulated 2,253 miles through seven of the United States, and never witnessed the tenth part of such hunger, hardships, and nakedness.

Now, my Lord, if the causes which I now lay before your Excellency, were not of very extraordinary importance, I would never presume that it should be laid before you.

But I consider myself in duty bound by charity to relieve distressed and hungry fellow-man.

Although I am sorry to state that my charity cannot extend further than to explain to the rich, where hunger and hardships exists, in almost in the greatest degree that nature can endure.

And which I shall endeavour to explain in detail, with all the truth and accuracy in my power, and that without the least exaggeration, as follows:—

There is about 4,000 persons in this parish, and all Catholics, and as poor as I shall describe, having among them no more than –

One cart,	No other school,
No wheel car,	One priest,
No coach, or any other vehicle,	No other resident gentleman,
One plough,	No bonnet,
Sixteen harrows,	No clock,
Eight saddles,	Three watches,
Two pillions,	Eight brass candlesticks,

Eleven bridles,
Twenty shovels,
Thirty-two rakes,
Seven table-forks,
Ninety-three chairs,
Two hundred and forty-three stools,
Ten iron grapes,
No swine, bogs, or pigs,
Twenty-seven geese,
Three turkeys,
Two feather beds,
Eight chaff beds,
Two stables,
Six cow houses,
One national school,

No looking glasses above 3d. in price,
No boots, no spurs,
No fruit trees,
No turnips,
No parsnips,
No carrots,
No clover,
Or any other garden vegetables, but potatoes and cabbage, and not more than ten square feet of glass in windows in the whole, with the exception of the chapel, the school house, the priest's house, Mr. Dombrain's house, and the constabulary brarrack.

None of their either married or unmarried woman can afford more than one shift, and the fewest number cannot afford any, and more than one half of both men and women cannot afford shoes to their feet, nor can many of them afford a second bed, but whole families of sons and daughters of mature age indiscriminately lying together with their parents, and all in the bare buff.

They have no means of harrowing their land, but with meadow rakes. Their Farms are so small that from four to ten farms can be harrowed in a day with one rake.

Their beds are straw – green and dried rushes or mountain bent: their bedclothes are either coarse sheets, or no sheets, and ragged filthy blankets.

And worse than all that I have mentioned, there is a general prospect of starvation, at the present prevailing among them, and that originating from various causes, but the principal cause is a rot or failure of seed in the last year's crop, together with a scarcity of winter forage, in consequence of a long continuation of storm since October last, in this part of the country.

So that they the people, were under the necessity of cutting down their potatoes and give them to their cattle to keep them alive. All these circumstances connected together, has brought hunger to reign among them to that degree, that the generality of the peasantry are on the small allowance of one meal a day, and many families cannot afford more than one meal in two days, and sometimes one meal in three days.

Their children crying and fainting with hunger, and their parents weeping, being full of grief, hunger, debility and dejection, with glooming aspect, looking at their children likely to expire in the jaws of starvation.

Also, in addition to all, their cattle and sheep are dying with hunger, and their owners forced by hunger to eat the flesh of such.

'Tis reasonable to suppose that the use of such flesh will raise some infectious disease among the people, and may very reasonably be supposed, that the people will die more numerous than the cattle and sheep, if some immediate relief are not sent to alleviate their hunger.

Now, my Lord, it may perhaps seem inconsistent with truth that all that I have said could possibly be true, but to convince your noble Excellency of the truth of all that I have said, I will venture to challenge the world to produce one single person to contradict any part of my statement.

Although I must acknowledge, that if reference were made to any of the landlords or landholders of the parish, that they would contradict it, as it is evident it would blast their honours if it were known abroad, that such a degree of want existed in their estates among their tenantry. But here is how I make my reference and support the truth of all that I have said; that is, if any unprejudiced gentleman should be sent here to investigate strictly into the truth of it; I will, if called on, go with him from house to house, where his eyes will fully satisfy and convince him, and where I can show him about one hundred and forty children bare naked, and was so during winter, and some hundreds only covered with filthy rags, most disgustful to look at. Also, man and beast housed together, *i.e.*, the families in one end of the house, and the cattle in the other end of the kitchen.

Some houses having within its walls, from One cwt. to Thirty cwts. of dung, others having from Ten to Fifteen tons weight of dung, and only cleaned out once a year!

Your most humble and obedient Servant,

PATRICK M'KYE.

A few one-roomed byre-houses built of mud-mortared field-stones are still standing, though no longer occupied,[12] but I found one inhabited by a bachelor and his ass and cow when I first visited the district in 1938. In 1837, out of about 700 houses, nearly all small farms, only six were provided with a separate cow-byre. They had no chimney and at best one small window without glass. The thatch was secured by heavy grass-ropes to which large stones were attached, hanging below the eaves. The new houses built by the tenants after the scattering had the benefit of lime-mortar and whitewash, and the luxury of a chimney, but living-conditions were little changed, and 'heaps of manure could still be seen at the bedside'. As late as 1911 the Congested Districts Board was offering princely grants of 30s. for 'the removal of livestock from the dwelling houses and converting the space occupied by them into an additional apartment'.[13]

The memorial of Patrick McKye leaves us in no doubt as to the extreme poverty and deprivation of the Gweedore district at the time when Lord George purchased the property: nor can there be any doubt about the demoralising consequences of illicit distilling. Conditions in the clustered clachans, moreover, must have favoured contagious diseases and there were endless wranglings over the minute subdivision of land and over trespassing. It is not easy to reconcile these terrible certainties with the idyllic picture painted later by many Irish writers who, in their attacks on landlordism, professed to see the years before the Famine as a time of innocent bliss and relative prosperity, romanticising the sorry business of the poteen makers and overlooking the degrading poverty and the bitterness of kinship disputes. These 'purest native Irish' says Holland, lived 'self-contained and self-contented, a peaceful pious unrepining race, using

and enjoying the land without let or hindrance'. According to Father
James McFadden, 'people were comfortable and happy in 1838'. Certainly
there were spiritual compensations. Even under these degrading conditions
the people of Gweedore seem to have retained a natural dignity and gaiety,
and their social gifts and conversational skills were quickened by the
throng of kinsmen and neighbours at crowded firesides.

They are great talkers; as firing is plentiful, they sit up half the night in winter,
talking and telling stories; they therefore dislike living in detached houses. They
are, however, a quiet, inoffensive race, when not interfered with, naturally civil
and kind in their manner. They seldom go out to labour on their farms till after
ten o'clock, when they have had their breakfast; and the spring and harvest time
are the only periods at which they exert themselves, and then they work very
hard; for the remainder of the year they are idle.

Hill pays tribute, however, to their intelligence, generosity and courage,
and a visitor after the Famine tells of 'recollections of nights of social
concourse, of aid in sickness, of sympathy in joy and sorrow, of combined
operations against bailiff or guager', though he also refers to their Celtic
'prejudices, insolence and obstinacy'.[14] Another fulsome recollection,
collected by the Irish Folklore Commission in the townland of Beltany,
is worth quoting in full.

There was no trade in the world then but come man of Beltany could try it –
the best weavers in the country were there; there were masons, carpenters,
coopers, thatchers and every kind of tradesmen you could name in this townland;
and after the famine years neither tale nor tidings of them was to be found.
They all went into strange and distant lands and never returned since. The
ruins of their houses were there until the land was divided and they were cleared
and fences made of the stones, leaving no trace of them to be seen now.[15]

Lord George began his formidable task by having a complete survey made
of his new property. 'It took about three years [1841–3] to accomplish the
divisions, as upwards of twenty thousand acres had to be thus arranged
and distributed.' Having visited the houses of all his tenants, he gave them
'notice to quit' and persuaded them to appoint a committee to assist him in
laying out the new farms, though he admits that opposition was 'vexatious
and harrowing'. As an encouragement he instituted a system of pre-
miums for improvements in crops, livestock and housing. Although some
of the new farms, cut out of the outfield or 'top-lands', conformed to the
improver's ideal rectangular shape, on the old infields the compromise
solution was the long strip farm. A strong advocate of the rectangular or
'squared' farm was Captain John Pitt Kennedy, whose model had been
followed by Sir Charles Style on the Cloghan estate near Stranorlar in
Glenfin, eastern Donegal, in reallotting rundale holdings and building
new houses with access roads in 1838.[16] Kennedy became secretary to the

Devon Commission, appointed in 1843 'to inquire into the state of the law and practice in respect to the occupation of land in Ireland'. The maps which he submitted to the Commission[17] to illustrate the rundale system (fig. 11), the landlord's proposed re-arrangement into separate squared farms (fig. 13), and the two-strip arrangement proposed by the tenants (fig. 12) are of the townland of Beltany Upper, in the Glenna River valley (on an estate adjoining Lord George Hill's). They are here reproduced from the 1845 edition of the pamphlet. The map of the townland today (fig. 14) shows that by and large the landlord had his way.

In trying to have their new holdings in two strips, one in each half of the townland, the tenants wished to perpetuate the principle of sharing portions of land of varying quality. Under this arrangement, too, they hoped to retain their clachans (fig. 12). Similarly Lord George's tenants wanted to be given their holdings in two strips when the land was redistributed, but the landlord compromised by giving them single strips.[18] Yet it seems that in the end they sometimes had their way, for the infield of a rundale community which I studied in 1938, at Glentornan on the former Gweedore estate, consisted of a small lake-side delta split into two halves, each of the six joint-tenants holding strips or sections of strips in both halves.[19] This had come about after 1847, when the revised first edition of the Ordnance Survey map shows only one set of strips. Evidently subdivision had occurred. In 1855, according to the Perambulation Books, rundale was still practised in several parts of the Gweedore estate. On the neighbouring Olphert estate, although the landlord claimed that he had abolished rundale in 1840, I found the old system in operation in 1938 in the little clachan of Meenacreevagh, in the townland of Beltany Mountain. Although now reduced to three families (1970), this tiny community is one of the last rundale relics in the district.

The inconvenience of the long strip farms is obvious. In extreme instances the strip might be several hundred yards long and no more than a few feet in width (one witness cited an example only seven or eight feet wide, so that the new houses had to be built lengthways instead of fronting the road in the new fashion). Again, a farm of four acres is quoted as being a mile long. Another disadvantage of the very long holdings was the amount of land wasted in fencing, which according to one landlord's estimate could amount to a quarter of the gross area. And the distances to be travelled in working the farm were calculated to be nearly four times those required on a squared farm.[20] That such disadvantages were accepted is a measure of the tenacity with which the tenants insisted on retaining some of the principles underlying the rundale system, for the long strips running up and down the hill slopes ensured that land of varying quality would be shared by all. Moreover, where the holdings were very narrow, the new houses built along the roadside were so close together that the advantages of community living were not sacrificed:

97

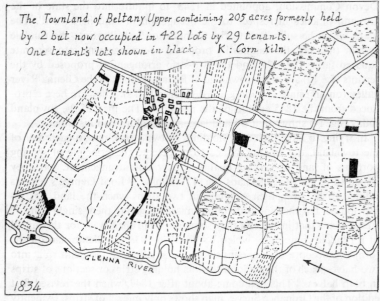

The Townland of Beltany Upper containing 205 acres formerly held by 2 but now occupied in 422 lots by 29 tenants. One tenant's lots shown in black. K : Corn kiln.

GLENNA RIVER

1834

Fig. 11.

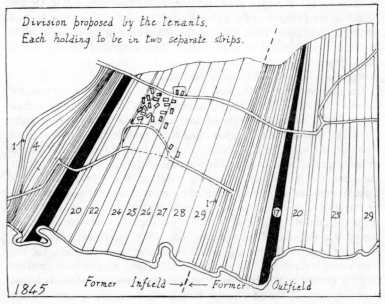

Division proposed by the tenants. Each holding to be in two separate strips.

1 4

20 22 24 25 26 27 28 29 17 20 25 29

1845

Former Infield → ← Former Outfield

Fig. 12.

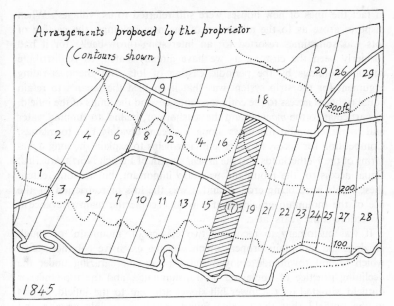

Arrangements proposed by the proprietor
(Contours shown)

1845

Fig. 13.

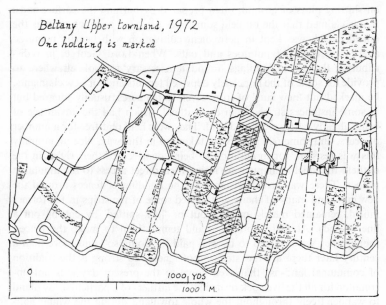

Beltany Upper townland, 1972
One holding is marked

Fig. 14.

in fact the lines of new houses were still referred to as 'villages'. When disputes arose as to the allocation of the new holdings, the casting of lots was sometimes resorted to; an interesting throw-back, for it had formerly been the custom, as we have already stated, to re-distribute rundale holdings by the periodic casting of lots. But the over-riding argument for the strip system was that it enabled the tenants to retain equal rights of access to the common lands beyond the limits of the infield, in particular to the *machair* and the seashore or, inland, to running water and to the common meadows along a stream dividing two townlands. Competition for access to water similarly helps to explain the long dyke-farms of the Netherlands and the *arpent* system of French North America. Equal access to 'the mountain' was also important, but to some extent these rights were being eroded, and it was the loss or restriction of the use of the mountain grazing that was to become the main grievance in Gweedore some years later.

It was customary to recognise two classes of 'mountain' or rough grazing: the mountain proper, which was the extensive commonage in which several townlands enjoyed rights of summer grazing under the declining practice of booleying or transhumance, and the top-lands or outfield, situated on the lower hill slopes adjacent to the infield. It was in the outfield that the tenants found readily accessible grazing and enjoyed rights of turbary, but it was also utilised to grow occasional crops on shifting plots of ground, often prepared by burning the surface sods. It was claimed that the outfield sometimes provided as much corn as the infield, which was kept in permanent cultivation with heavily manured alternating crops of potatoes and oats. When Lord George, in redistributing the infield holdings, found it necessary to look elsewhere to provide for some of the hopelessly deprived tenants and for new claimants, he marked out 'new cuts' of from seven to ten acres, usually squared but in some instances striped,[21] in the outfield, which had the advantage of being already partly reclaimed land. They were held rent-free for a number of years, and some 600 acres were taken up in this way. Not unnaturally this was resisted, for in addition to being deprived of their rights in the outfield the infield tenants were losing their direct access to the mountain proper. There was great resistance to the building of fences around the new cuts, and many of them, and indeed some of the strips in the former infield, remained merely marked out or 'lock-spitted' by cutting out a line of sods. At first, 'nothing would tempt them to make the fences, though they were offered to be well paid for doing so', and more than a century later there are few stock-proof fences. So strong is the tradition of communal land-use that even down to the present day it is not uncommon for all the livestock owned by the farmers of a particular townland to wander freely throughout the whole townland during the winter half-year.

But the most persistent grievance was the restriction placed by the landlord on the use of the mountain pastures, located mainly on the western slopes of the Tievelehid massif and on the hills to the south-west of Lough Nacung. In 1841 Lord George had reserved 12,000 acres of mountain grazing – nearly half the area of the entire estate – for his own use, employing two herds to look after his livestock. There were no fences, however, and any cattle found straying on the portion thus 'stolen by the landlord' were impounded. Matters came to a head when in 1855 he let portions of the mountain to Scottish graziers who imported large numbers of sheep. The tenants complained that they had no grazing land 'except the ridges, waste patches and roadsides', although the landlord claimed that every townland was allowed 'a definite area of mountain grazing'. In the following years many hundreds of sheep were stolen or killed – according to one account there was a loss of 1130 sheep in 1857[22] – and in 1858 a Select Committee of the House of Commons was appointed to look into the complaints. As a consequence the Grand Jury imposed a sheep tax and a police tax to cover the losses and to meet the cost of police protection. There were complaints that the tenantry were worse off than they had been even in the famine years, and in the same year (1858) ten priests drew up an eloquent appeal and sent a petition to parliament which resulted in the appointment of a Parliamentary Committee of Enquiry. The appeal runs as follows:

In the wilds of Donegal, down in the bogs and glens of Gweedore and Clough-aneely, thousands and thousands of human beings, made after the image and likeness of God, are perishing, or next to perishing, amid squalidness and misery, for want of food and clothing, far away from aid and pity. On behalf of these famishing victims of oppression and persecution, we appeal for sub-stantial assistance to enable us to relieve their wretchedness, and rescue them from death and starvation.

There are at this moment 800 families subsisting on seaweed, crabs, cockles, or any other edible matter they can pick up along the seashore or scrape off the rocks. There araboute 600 adults of both sexes, who through sheer poverty are now going barefoot, amid the inclemency of the season, on this bleak northern coast. There are about 700 families that have neither bed nor bedclothes . . . Thousands of the male population have only one cotton shirt; while thousands have not even one. There are about 600 families who have neither cow, sheep, nor goat and who . . . hardly know the taste of milk or butter.

This fine old Celtic race is about being crushed to make room for Scotch and English sheep.[23]

The money collected, amounting to about £600, was used, according to one account, to compensate those on whom the police and sheep taxes had been levied rather than for general relief.[24] The priests pretended that the weather and the Scottish herders were responsible for the loss of sheep: 'the strange sheep imported to these mountains throve not. Last winter was very prejudicial to sheep, particularly under Scotch treatment.'[25]

The Report of the Select Committee on Destitution in Gweedore and Cloughaneely contains harrowing accounts of the conditions under which many of the tenants were living, but the committee found no evidence of destitution and concluded that the complaints were much exaggerated and that the prevailing poverty was not attributable to the landlords. It recommended emigration as a solution, but seasonal emigration was too strongly entrenched among the coastal communities. Those giving evidence for the tenants stated that conditions were worse than they had been in the famine years or before the coming of Lord George Hill, while the landlords claimed that conditions had improved and that the appearance of poverty was 'dressed up' to impress the enquiring committee, supplies of food being hidden and cattle driven off. They admitted that the houses were 'comfortless', but that 'the people seem to have less regard for comfort than those of any other part of Ireland' and that the dwelling of a man worth £400 was as wretched as the rest.[26] 'Rags and poor living' were 'more a fashion than a necessity, not to be regarded as real indications of poverty'.[27] The committee looked carefully into the alleged dependence on seaweed for food, particularly on *Dulaman* or 'sweet sea-weed' (the tips of *Fucus vesiculosus*, bladder wrack). There is no doubt that some varieties of seaweed were normally eaten, and indeed relished, as 'kitchen' to liven up a dish of potatoes, but though potatoes at times became 'kitchen' to the seaweed one cannot help feeling that, as happened later on when Mr George Trevelyan, the Chief Secretary, visited Donegal in 1883, 'all sorts of tableaux were arranged for the inspectors, including a family taking a meal of seaweed'.[28] There certainly was great poverty, and agitation persisted.

A question of general interest which arises is the apparent anomaly of the existence in this depressed area of the Ulster Custom of tenant right, which is believed to have originated in the special circumstances of the Ulster plantation, when protestant settlers built their houses and improved their holdings at their own expense.[29] The Ulster Custom not only gave tenants some security of tenure but, it is generally held, 'promoted a spirit of manliness and independence and encouraged industry and respect for the law'. The practice apparently spread to Roman Catholic areas and to joint-tenancies, where its effects were less fortunate. It is conceivable, however, that the custom may have been based on the rights of clansmen in pre-plantation times.[30] Although there was no inducement to make improvements under the rundale system, with so much land held in common, the sums paid when holdings changed hands were high, amounting in Gweedore, in 1838, to anything from fifteen to thirty times the annual rent. Sales of holdings, however, are likely to have been few before emigration set in on a considerable scale: half a century later the figures had risen to forty to 130 years' purchase. It was not so much payment for improvements made, however, as for the good-will, and it not only co-existed with extreme poverty but seems to have contributed to it. Land being almost the sole means of support, people would beggar themselves to possess it, and could not afford to buy livestock or seed. Yet because of the Ulster Custom the tenants, although they held the land only from year to year, felt they were part owners and they were very jealous of their rights. The appropriation of common pastures, as we have seen, was a major source of grievance. By the time of Lord George's death, hopes of complete peasant ownership had already been raised by the passing in 1870 of the first of the many Land Acts, though the transference of ownership did not take place in many instances until the present century. In the west the most effective agencies were the Congested Districts Board, established under the Balfour Act in 1891, the Estates Commissioners, and the Land Commission, to whom it fell to redistribute those farms, particularly in Co. Mayo, which were still held in rundale after 1922.

The Land Act of 1870 which legalised the Ulster Custom had afforded tenants no protection against rising rents, and those who failed to pay them were still faced with eviction. In reply to charges levelled against him, however, Hill claimed that he had served no ejection notices and that 'in no instance was a tenant dispossessed of his farm'. Other Donegal landlords were not so generous: indeed some of the most notorious evictions had occurred on the Adare estate at Glenveagh in the winter of 1860–61. In Gweedore Lord George not unnaturally lost some of his improving zeal in his old age, when agitation was reaching its height. After his death in 1879 it was his successor, Captain Arthur Hill, who bore the brunt of the land war. By this time the Land and Home Rule had become the main themes of nationalist politics. It was in 1879 that the National Land League was founded in Dublin by Michael Davitt, its aim being to fight for rent reductions and in the long run for peasant proprietorship. It advocated the witholding of labour and rents and the use of the boycott, so called from an incident in Co. Mayo in 1878.

In 1886, with the defeat of the first Home Rule bill, the League inaugurated a Plan of Campaign to implement its policies, and Father James McFadden, 'the Patriot Priest of Gweedore', who had been Chairman of the League since 1882 (its first chairman had been Parnell) led the Plan of Campaign in Donegal and began by enforcing a boycott on the Gweedore Hotel. There were many prosecutions for offences committeed in connection with the Campaign, and Father McFadden was imprisoned for six months in 1888 for encouraging non-payment of rents and boycotting. On his release he continued his activities and was again arrested.

It was after he had conducted mass at Derrybeg chapel on Sunday, 2 February 1889, that 'the Gweedore artillery', an angry mob armed with sticks and stones, battered to death District Inspector Martin, who had come to arrest him, on the steps of the priest's house. This was the climax of the troubles, and Gweedore soon ceased to occupy the prominent place it had held in Irish affairs for almost half a century.

Today the visitor will see many traces of Lord George Hill's work: I have referred to his derelict hotel, but more conspicuous are his improvements at Bunbeg harbour. One of his first tasks had been to build a corn store and a corn-drying kiln at the mouth of the Clady River in 1839. By providing a local market for grain he hoped to curb the activities of the gombeen men and to check illicit distillation. A quay was built to accommodate vessels which began to trade with Glasgow, Liverpool and Dublin, and a general merchandise store was erected. This is at present being converted into a quay-side hotel, but much of the original structure survives, including the inscription in Irish – taken from the Psalms – over the entrance. In 1845 a corn mill was added, and being fitted with French burr-stones it was able to grind Indian corn for relief during the famine years. A saw mill and flax mill were built later. All this was the work of a man who, according to his enemies, 'was determined to exterminate the whole Irish race'.[31]

Lord George died at Ballyar on 6 April 1879 and is buried in Letterkenny churchyard. In the church by the Clady Bridge at Bunbeg is a memorial tablet to this 'Self Denying Christian' who 'devoted his life and fortune to civilise Gweedore, and to raise its people to a higher social and moral level'.

Its people resolutely refused to accept his brand of civilisation, but they reluctantly submitted to changes in agricultural practice, land-use and settlement; and Lord George's most enduring memorial is the human landscape which he helped to mould. But even here the Irish have had their way. The road from Gweedore River to the Bloody Foreland, some eight miles long, today resembles a vast linear clachan, deriving such form as it has from the siting of the roadside houses, new and old, on the narrow strips of land which were, ironically, designed to break up the old rundale clusters.

Innovation in Ireland has repeatedly spread from the east and south of the island towards the north-west – north Connacht and Donegal. The relict-features described in *Facts from Gweedore* are part of a complex of cultural survivals persisting in this far corner of Ireland, isolated from the rest of the country by bold mountain ridges of quartzite and granite. It is an area of great interest to students of the Gaelic language, and to collectors of its rich oral literature. It shares with Tory island the primitive paddle-curragh, and Tory has preserved also in unusual form a rundale-derived landholding system with bilateral inheritance rights which retains the clachan.[32] Dr McCourt, discussing such elements of material culture in north-western Ireland as the bed outshot and the cruck-derived coupled roof-truss, has suggested that they may once have been much more widely distributed.[33] Recently, too, Dr Alan Gailey has analysed another traditional element in the rural economy of the north-west – the communal corn-drying kiln – which he considers to be yet another relict feature finding its last foothold here in the far north-west.[34]

Notes

CHAPTER I: *Habitat, heritage and history: an anthropogeographic view* (pp. 1–17)

1. J. Huxley, in G. Wolstenholme (ed.), *Man and his Future* (London, 1963).
2. J.C. Beckett, *The Making of Modern Ireland 1603–1923* (London, 1966), p. 263.
3. J.R. Green, *The Making of England* (London, 1881), p. vii.
4. R.G. Collingwood, *The Idea of History* (Oxford, 1946), p. 277.
5. W. Stokes, *The Life of George Petrie* (London, 1868), p. 24.
6. Cf. P.W. Joyce, *A Child's History of Ireland* (Dublin, 1897). Joyce claimed that he wrote 'in a broad and just spirit' and that 'for the first and only time he had brought within the reach of the general public a knowledge of the whole social life of Ancient Ireland'. It was a romantic view, designed to counteract the prevailing English view of ancient Ireland as a barbarous country; and he and his imitators did much to promote an image of Ireland as a land of saints and scholars which had been fashioned by warlike but cultivated and loveable Celtic heroes.
7. E.E. Evans-Pritchard, *The Nuer* (Oxford, 1940), p. 85.
8. S.F. Markham, *Climate and the Energy of Nations* (London, 1944), p. 131.
9. Lord Raglan, *How came Civilisation?* (London, 1939), p. 12.
10. J.T. Glacken, *Traces on the Rhodian Shore* (Berkeley, 1967).
11. H.J. Fleure, *The Trilogy of the humanities in education* (Aberystwyth, 1918). Compare the comment of Lucien Febvre on Professor Roger Dion, 'qui cache des trésors dans les lieux secrets'. Ref. in J.L.M. Gulley, 'The practice of historical geography', *Tidschrift von Econ. en Soc. Geog.* (1961), 169–83.
12. I am indebted to Professor Quinn for allowing me to quote from the MS. of an unpublished lecture entitled 'Is British History necessary?' delivered in Liverpool at the Historical Association Conference, 20 April 1968.
13. I am grateful to Professor Gary Dunbar for letting me see a copy of his forthcoming paper on 'Some Exegetical notes on the concept of Geographical Personality'.
14. L. Febvre, *La Terre et l'Evolution humaine* (Paris, 1922), p. 364.
15. F. Braudel, *La Mediterranée à l'Epoque de Phillipe II* (Paris, 1949), p. xiii.
16. X. de Planhol, 'Le Chien de Berger', *Bull. de l'Assoc. de Géographes Français*, 370 (1969), 355–68.
17. F. Braudel wrote the preface to *Villages désertés et histoire économique, XIe–XVIIIe siecles,* (Paris, 1965).
18. K.H. Connell, *The Population of Ireland, 1750–1845* (Oxford, 1950).
19. R.E. Glasscock, 'Moated sites and deserted boroughs and villages', in N. Stephens and R.E. Glasscock (eds.), *Irish Geographical Studies* (Belfast, 1970), pp. 162–77.
20. F.P. Jones, 'The Gwerin of Wales', in G. Jenkins (ed.), *Studies in Folk Life* (London 1969), p. 4.
21. J.C. Beckett, *The Study of Irish History* (Belfast, 1963), p. 17.
22. T.W. Moody, 'A New History of Ireland', *Irish Historical Studies*, 16 (1969), 3.
23. Cf. T.W. Moody and F.X. Martin, *The Course of Irish History* (Cork, 1967). It must be said, however, that this admirable collection of twenty-one television lectures, while mainly political in tone, goes some way to meet the criticism that Irish historiography has neglected prehistory, protohistory and social history, and the first lecture, 'A geographer's view of Ireland' by

J.H. Andrews, treats geography as a continuing factor in history. An earlier work on the Great Famine (Edwards and Williams (eds.), 1956) is enriched and illuminated by a chapter by Professor Roger McHugh, which makes extensive use of oral material.

CHAPTER II: *The Irish habitat* (pp. 18–41)

1. I owe the term to Professor A.H. Clark, whose *Acadia* (Wisconsin, 1968) is an admirable treatment of the historical geography of Nova Scotia down to 1760.
2. G.A.J. Cole, *Ireland the Outpost* (Oxford, 1919), p. 7.
3. H.J. Mackinder, *Britain and the British Seas*, 2nd ed. (Oxford, 1922), p. 15.
4. R.A.S. Macalister, *Ancient Ireland* (London, 1935), p. 281.
5. D. Linton, 'Tertiary landscape evolution', in J.W. Watson and J.B. Sissons (eds.), *The British Isles* (Edinburgh, 1964).
6. H. Case, 'Settlement patterns in the North Irish Neolithic', *Ulster J. Archaeol.* 32 (1969), 3.
7. T. Jones Hughes, 'Town and Baile in Irish Place-names', in Stephens and Glasscock (eds.) (1970), fig. 15.4.
8. W.H. Hudson, *A Traveller in Little Things* (London, 1921), p. 85.
9. N. Robertson, *Crowned Harp* (Dublin, 1960), p. 47.
10. I am reminded of the name given locally to a very fat drumlin situated on the edge of Ronaldsway Airport, near the ecclesiastical centre of Castletown, Isle of Man. It is 'the bishop's belly'.
11. P. Kavanagh, *The Green Fool* (London, 1938), p. 12.
12. E.E. Evans, 'The Personality of Ulster', *Trans. Inst. Brit. Geographers*, 51 (1970), 15.
13. Macalister, *Ancient Ireland*, p. 280.
14. D.A. Binchy, 'Secular Institutions', in M. Dillon (ed.), *Early Irish Society* (Dublin, 1954), p. 52.
15. A. Smith, 'Vegetational and climatic history of Ireland', in Stephens and Glasscock (eds.) (1970), p. 83.
16. G.F. Mitchell, 'Post-boreal pollen diagrams from Irish raised bogs', *Proc. Roy. Irish Acad.* 57 (1956), 242.
17. Professor Quinn's work, *The Elizabethans and the Irish* (Ithaca, 1966) is exceptional in making good use of archaeological and ethnological data. See also A.C. Forbes, 'Some legendary and historical references to Irish woods, and their significance', *Proc. Roy. Irish Acad.* 41 (1932), 15–36.
18. J.W. Watson, 'Forest or bog; man the deciding factor', *Scot. Geog. Mag.* 55 (1939), 153.
19. W. Fitzgerald, *Historical Geography of early Ireland* (London, 1925), p. 48.
20. Dr John Cooney, in a Report on Alcoholism (see *The Irish Times*, 21 September 1971) states that over ten per cent of total personal spending in the Irish Republic is on alcohol, and that the main cause is 'depression'.
21. M.J. Gardiner and P. Ryan, 'A new generalised Soil Map of Ireland', *Irish J. Agric. Research*, 8 (1969), 95–109.
22. E.E. Evans, *Irish Folk Ways* (London, 1957), p. 131. A striking example of Irish sensitivity and ingenuity is the denial, against all the evidence, that the practice ever existed. It is argued by J.J. McAuliffe, 'Ploughing by horses' tails', *The Irish Book Lover*, 29 (1943), 9–11, that the English invented this Irish vice and that the sole purpose of the laws passed against it since the seventeenth century was to prove that it must have existed. In fact the custom was not so barbarous as might be thought.
23. In fact they have been recorded before. The earliest reference I know is in a letter from the Archbishop of Dublin published in Thomas Molyneux's edition of Gerard Boate, *A Natural History of Ireland* (Dublin, 1755), p. 163. The recent discoveries are in Co. Mayo. See M. Herity, *Irish University Review* (Spring, 1971), 258–61. See Note 44, Chapter III.

CHAPTER III: *The Irish heritage* (pp. 42–65)

1. F.R. Leavis and D. Thompson, *Culture and Environment* (London, 1937), p. 1.
2. M. Hooper, 'Dating Hedges', *Area*, 4 (1970), 63–5.
3. F.W. Maitland, *Domesday Book and Beyond* (Cambridge, 1907) p. 16.
4. J.C. Zeuss, *Grammatica Celtica* (Leipzig, 1853).
5. C.S. Coon, *The Races of Europe* (New York, 1939), pp. 376–84, considers that at least half the genetic ancestry of the composite modern Irishman is to be referred to the survival of strains from the oldest (Mesolithic) settlers. A.E. Hooton and C.W. Dupertuis, *The Physical Anthropology of Ireland* (Cambridge Mass, 1955) are more cautious. They searched, however, for the supposed 'Celtic' type and found it uncommon among native Gaelic speakers, and best represented down the east coast.
6. E. Hackett and M.E. Folan, 'ABO and RH Blood groups of the Aran Islands', *Irish J. Medical Science*, 390 (1958), 247–61. The A frequency for the Aran Islands is given as 40 per cent, the O, 50. These figures resemble those for eastern Ireland. Averages for western Ireland are A, 26.5; O, 60. The available figures for Northern Ireland are A, 33; O, 55.
7. D. Greene, *The Irish Language* (Dublin, 1966), p. 61.
8. H. Wagner, 'The Origin of the Celts', *Philolog. Trans.* (1969), 206.
9. B. Adams, 'Language and Man in Ireland', *Ulster Folklife*, 15/16 (1970), 152.
10. Wagner, *Philolog. Trans.* 208. Linguistic scholars differ in their views on the affinities between these languages. A bold attempt to explain them will be found in Nils M. Holmer, Ants Uesson and Olof Smedberg, 'On Linguistic Types, Blood Groups and Culture Areas', *Sprakliga Bidrag*, 4, no. 16 (1961), 5–29. This exercise in correlation, with maps intended 'to give a mere sketch of the development without detail', can be criticised by specialists but it is a refreshing cross-disciplinary approach to an interpretation of world distributions. In a more recent paper ('The principal linguistic types', *Arsbok* (1967–8), 184–91) Holmer restricts himself to a discussion of his four types of world languages, based on structural patterns.
11. A. Ross, *Pagan Celtic Britain* (London, 1967), p. 201. Professor Greene tells me, however, that the Irish warriors campaigned on spring water: they got drunk afterwards.
12. *Ibid.* p. 61. Cf. the various contributions to J. Ryan (ed.), *Saint Patrick* (Dublin, 1958).
13. A.T. Lucas, 'Plundering of Churches in Ireland', in E. Rynne (ed.), *North Munster Studies* (Limerick 1967), pp. 172–229.
14. Cf. M. Tierney (ed.), *Daniel O'Connell: nine centenary essays* (Dublin, 1945), p. 151. 'To conceive of our history as having been guided by one true doctrine, the doctrine of Nationality... is to make nonsense of a great part of our history.' It could be argued that by adopting the Anglo-Irish concept of the nation the Irish committed themselves to a West European culture-form for which neither habitat nor heritage had fitted them. One doubts whether the Irish version of British parliamentary democracy and its tools and trappings – a bureaucratic civil service and what is sometimes called a 'filing cabinet', a flag and a national anthem – are really at home in a country where familial and religious affiliations are so strong.
15. K. Jackson, *The oldest Irish Tradition* (Cambridge, 1964), p. 13.
16. P.L. Henry, 'Anglo-Irish Word-charts', in *Ulster Dialects* (Ulster Folk Museum, 1964), p. 147.
17. M. MacNeill, *The Festival of Lughnasa* (London, 1962).
18. E.C. Amoroso and P.A. Jewell, 'The exploitation of the milk-ejection reflex by primitive peoples', in A.E. Mourant and F.E. Zeuner (eds.), *Man and Cattle* (Roy. Anthrop. Inst., 1963).
19. E.E. Evans, *Prehistoric and Early Christian Ireland* (London, 1966), p. 11.
20. J.M. Coles, 'Some Irish Horns of the late Bronze Age', *J. Roy. Soc. Antiq. Ireland*, 97 (1967), 113–17.
21. A. ApSimon, 'The earlier Bronze Age', *Ulster J. Archaeol.* 32 (1970), 28–72.
22. P. Harbinson, 'Irish Early Bronze Age associated finds', *Proc. Roy. Irish*

Acad. 67 (1968), 35–91, and *Die Prähistorische Bronzefunde Europas*, 6 (Munich, 1969(1)), 1.

23. Wagner, *Philolog. Trans.* 229.
24. P. Harbinson, 'Celtic funerary tradition', in O.-H. Frey (ed.), *Festschrift Dehn* (Bonn, 1969(2)).
25. Evans, *Irish Folk Ways*, p. 297.
26. J. McEvoy, *Statistical Survey of the county of Tyrone* (Dublin, 1802), p. 69.
27. A. Nicholson, *Ireland's Welcome to the Stranger* (London, 1847), p. 397.
28. E.E. Evans, 'Some Survivals of the Irish openfield system', *Geography*, 24 (1939), 24–36.
29. See however A.J. Otway-Ruthven, 'Organisation of Anglo-Norman agriculture in the Middle Ages', *J. Roy. Soc. Antiq. Ireland*, 81 (1951), 1–13.
30. D. McCourt, 'The dynamic quality of Irish rural settlement', in Buchanan *et al.* (eds.), *Man and his Habitat* (London, 1971), pp. 126–64.
31. R.H. Buchanan, 'Common fields and enclosure', *Ulster Folklife*, 15/16 (1970), 99–118. See also Buchanan, 'Rural Settlement in Ireland', in Stephens and Glasscock (eds.) (1970).
32. F.H.A. Aalen, 'The Origins of Enclosures in eastern Ireland', in Stephens and Glasscock (eds.) (1970).
33. Binchy, 'Secular Institutions', p. 54.
34. M. Duignan, 'Irish Agriculture in early historic times', *J. Roy. Soc. Antiq. Ireland*, 74 (1944), 4.
35. J.H. Clapham and Eileen Power (eds.), *The Cambridge Economic History of Europe*, vol. 1. *The Agrarian Life of the Middle Ages* (Cambridge, 1941), p. 161.
36. J.J. O'Meara, *The Topography of Ireland by Giraldus Cambrensis* (Dundalk, 1951), p. 85.
37. Evans, *Irish Folk Ways*, ch. 2; D. McCourt, 'Infield and Outfield in Ireland', *Econ. Hist. Rev.* 7 (1954–5), 369–76, and 'The dynamic quality of Irish rural settlement' (1971).
38. A. Gailey, 'The Typology of the Irish Spade' and C.O. Danachair, 'The sue of the spade in Ireland', in Gailey and Fenton (eds.), *The Spade in Northern and Atlantic Europe* (Ulster Folk Museum, 1970).
39. Similarly among Gaelic freeholders the periodic reallocation of land under the system of inheritance to which the English gave the name 'gavelkind' led to many disputes. The fact that close kinsmen were involved made them all the more bitter. This was a fatal weakness of the Irish system of inheritance at all levels of society: 'The course of dynastic history in Ireland reeks with bloodshed disorder and internecine war': G.A. Hayes-McCoy, 'Gaelic Society in Ireland in the late sixteenth century', *Historical Studies*, 4 (1963), 57, quoting Professor J. Hogan.
40. J. Graham, 'Rural Society in Connacht, 1600–1640', in Stephens and Glasscock (eds.) (1970).
41. J. Graham 'Transhumance in Ireland', *Adv. Science*, 37 (1953), 74–9.
42. E.E. Evans, 'Donegal Harvest', *Ulster Folklife*, 14 (1968), 3–5.
43. These discoveries by Mr Seán Nualláin await publication.
44. M. Herity, 'Prehistoric fields in Ireland', *Irish University Review* (Spring, 1971), 258–61. See Note 23, Chapter II. The letter from the Archbishop of Dublin, c. 1750, referring to the presence of ridges and furrows in the wild mountains adds, 'In truth there are few places but either visibly or when the bogs are removed there remain marks of the plough.' Similarly Silvester O'Halloran (*A General History of Ireland*, 2 vols. (London, 1778), vol. 1, p. 101) states: 'The summits of the most dreary mountains at this day, and most of the bogs in the kingdom when gone to a certain depth, exhibit lively traces of the plough and the harrow.'
45. S.P.O' Riordain, 'Lough Gur Excavations', *Proc. Roy. Irish Acad.* 56 (1954), 297–459.
46. E.E Evans, 'The Atlantic Ends of Europe', *Adv. Science*, 15 (1958), 54–64. See also H. Uhlig, 'Old hamlets in Western and Central Europe', *Geografiska Annaler*, 43 (1961), 285–312. For a comparative survey of Atlantic field systems

see P. Flatrès, *Géographie rurale de quatre contrées Celtiques* (Rennes, 1957). The contrast between these two complexes – openfields, long plough strips and villages: infield/outfield, irregular plots (sometimes with enclosure) and single farms or hamlets – between 'la grande culture' and 'la petite culture', has absorbed the attention of many French economic historians and historical geographers since Marc Bloch and Roger Dion, who saw the contrast reflected in 'collective mentalities, social and even juridical types'. They have failed to find an explanation of the two systems and their distribution by reference to single sources, whether habitat, heritage or conventional history.

47. Evans, *Trans. Inst. Brit. Geographers*, 51 (1970) 3.
48. A.T. Lucas, 'Paring and Burning in Ireland', in Gailey and Fenton (eds.) (1970), pp. 99–154.
49. A. Campbell, 'Notes on the Irish House', *Folkliv* (1937), 222.
50. G.A. Hayes-McCoy, *Scots Mercenary Forces in Ireland, 1565–1603* (London, 1937).
51. Some of the humbler houses shown in early seventeenth-century illustrations of the plantations of the London Companies in County Londonderry seem to be of this central chimney type.
52. S. Erixon, 'West European connections and culture relations', *Folkliv* (1938), 137–72.

CHAPTER IV: *The Personality of Ireland* (pp. 66–84)

1. C.O. Sauer, 'The Personality of Mexico', in J. Leighley (ed.), *Landscape and Life: a selection from the writings of Carl Ortwin Sauer* (Berkeley, 1965), p. 117.
2. Cf. G. Daniel, 'The Personality of Wales' in I. Ll. Foster and L. Alcock (eds.), *Culture and Environment* (London, 1963). For an architectural interpretation see M. Craig, *The Personality of Leinster*, (Dublin, 1961; reprinted 1971).
3. Cf. C. Kluckhohn, 'South-western studies of culture and personality', *American Anthropologist*, 56 (1954), 685–708.
4. Mr Noel Hamilton tells me that these names were taken from the titles of patriotic Gaelic songs of the eighteenth century: Róisén Dubh and Caitlín Ní Uallacháin. Other names for Ireland were taken from legendary princesses, among them Eriu (Eire).
5. R. Flower, *The Irish Tradition* (Oxford, 1947), p. 1.
6. D. Greene, 'Early Irish Literature', in M. Dillon (ed.) (1954), p. 34.
7. Sir Ernest Barker (ed.), *The Character of England* (Oxford, 1947).
8. A. Toynbee, *A Study of History*, 12 vols., vol. 2 (London, 1934), p. 100.
9. J. Beddoe, *The Races of Britain* (London, 1885; reprinted 1971), p. 291. More recent anthropometric studies recognise a tall heavy and rather broad-headed type as having a strong mesolithic strain. Men of this stock from south-western Ireland have won a reputation as navvies, but it can also, to judge from portraits, produce a Daniel O'Connell.
10. M.J. O'Kelly, 'Excavations and experiments in ancient Irish cooking-places', *J. Roy. Soc. Antiq. Ireland*, 84 (1954), 105–55.
11. Evans, *Irish Folk Ways*, p. 233.
12. Case, *Ulster J. Archaeol.* 32 (1969), 7.
13. R. de Valera, 'The Court Cairns of Ireland', *Proc. Roy. Irish Acad.* 60 (1960), 9–140.
14. E.E. Evans, 'The Peasant and the Past', *Adv. Science*, 17 (1960), 293–302. It is not easy to find a satisfactory definition of a peasant, but in so far as the world's peasantries are regarded as 'part societies' associated, as in medieval Europe, with urban systems, it is doubtful whether the word can properly be applied to Gaelic Ireland until recent centuries. An index of the spread of peasant attitudes in Ireland during the Middle Ages may perhaps be found in the diffusion of the cult of the Virgin Mother. I cannot find that

Irish historians have interested themselves in these anthropogeographical correlations.

15. H.J. Fleure, 'Prehistoric elements in our heritage', *Bull. John Rylands Lib.* 18 (1934), 36.
16. M. Bloch, *Feudal Society* (London, 1961), p. xiv.
17. J. Kelleher, 'Early Irish history and pseudo-history', *Studia Hibernica*, 3 (1963), 116.
18. Despite an astonishing facility of speech, Flower, *The Irish Tradition*, p. 110 regards a concrete cast of language and 'an epigrammatic concision' as essentially Irish qualities.
19. E.G. Bowen, *Saints, Seaways and Settlements in the Celtic Lands* (Cardiff, 1969).
20. Greene, 'Early Irish Literature' (1954) p. 85.
21. *Ibid.* p. 35.
22. J. Ryan, *Irish Monasticism* (Dublin, 1931) p. 299. Ryan also regarded St Patrick's selection of Armagh as an accident. For general views more in line with the present writer's see M. and L. de Paor (1958) and Hughes (1966).
23. Kelleher, *Studia Hibernica*, 3 (1963), 118.
24. See his Rhind Lectures (Society of Antiquaries of Scotland, 1971–2) on 'Cattle in ancient and medieval Irish society'.
25. Kelleher, *Studia Hibernica*, 3 (1963), 127.
26. O'Meara, *The Topography of Ireland*, p. 85.
27. D. Gwynn, in Tierney (ed.) (1949), p. 172.
28. Ryan, *Irish Monasticism*, p. 215.
29. Kavanagh, *The Green Fool*, p. 38.
30. T. Colby, *Memoir of the City and North Western Liberties of Londonderry* (Dublin, 1837), Introduction.
31. Stokes, *George Petrie*, p. 89.
32. Y. Goblet, *La Transformation de la Géographie politique de l'Irlande au XVIIe siècle*, 2 vols. (Paris, 1930), vol. 2, p. 355.
33. *Analecta Hibernica*, 2 (1931), 51.
34. S.O. Nualláin and R. de Valera, *Survey of the Megalithic Tombs of Ireland*, vol. 1 *County Clare* (Dublin, 1961), p. 108.
35. Evans, *Irish Folk Ways*, p. 37.
36. D.B. Quinn, 'Sir Thomas Smith and the beginnings of English colonial theory', *Proc. Amer. Philosoph. Soc.* 89 (1945), 546.
37. M.W. Heslinga, *The Irish Border as a cultural divide* (Assen, 1962; reprinted 1971), p. 101. A refreshing geographical approach by another continental scholar to Irish political history will be found in E. Rumpf, *Nationalismus und Sozialismus in Irland* (Heidelberg, 1959). An English edition (*Nationalism and Social Change*) is being prepared by Dr A.C. Hepburn for publication by the Institute of Irish Studies.
38. F. Young, *Ireland at the Crossroads* (London, 1903), p. 120.
39. L. Durrell, *The Spirit of Place* (London, 1969), p. 156.
40. A. Lomax, *Folk Song Style and Culture* (Amer. Ass. Adv. Science, 1969).

APPENDIX: *Facts from Gweedore* (pp. 85–105)

1. Mrs Craik, 'An Unknown Country', *The English Illustrated Magazine* (1887), 477–558.
2. D. Holland, *The Landlord in Donegal* (Belfast, n.d. [1857–8],) p. 74.
3. S. Gwynn, *Highways and Byways in Donegal and Antrim* (London, 1899; 1928 edition), pp. 131, 142.
4. T. Carlyle, *Reminiscences of my Irish Journey in 1849* (London, 1882), pp. 236–62.
5. *Congested Districts Board: Base-line Reports* (1891–95), section 5, Gweedore.
6. F.H. Aalen and H. Brody, *Gola: the Life and Last Days of an Island Community* (Cork, 1969), p. 30.

7. T.W. Freeman, 'The Changing Distribution of Population in Donegal', *Journ. of Statistical and Social Enquiry Soc. of Ireland,* 17 (1939–40), 1–12.
8. *Report on Destitution*, p. 134 (*Report from the Select Committee on Destitution, Gweedore and Cloughaneely*, H.C. 412 1857–8). A cow's grass is a unit of grazing capacity, not of area. In other parts of Ireland it is known as a sum, collop or gneeve. On the number of cow's grasses held depends the number of cattle (or their equivalent in other stock) that can use the common pastures.
9. J. McParlan, *Statistical Survey of the County of Donegal* (Dublin, 1802), p. 64.
10. J. McFadden, *The Present and Past of the Agrarian Struggle in Gweedore* (Londonderry, 1889).
11. *Congested Districts Board, 19th Report* (1911), Cd. 5712, 9.
12. D. McCourt, 'The House with Bedroom over Byre: a Long-house derivative?' *Ulster Folklife*, 15/16 (1970), 3–19, fig. 1. See also E.E. Evans, 'Donegal Survivals', *Antiquity* 13 (1939), 207–22.
13. *Congested Districts Board, 19th Report* (1911), 9.
14. *Dublin University Magazine*, 41 (1853), 9–22.
15. Quoted in R.D. Edwards and T.D. Williams (eds.) *The Great Famine* (Dublin, 1956) p. 434.
16. Mr and Mrs S.C. Hall, *Ireland* (1841–3). New edition (*c.* 1870), vol. 1, p. 261.
17. *Digest of Evidence taken before Her Majesty's Commissioners on Occupation of Land in Ireland* (The Devon Commission). Prepared by J.P. Kennedy. Part I (1847), p. 422.
These maps were reproduced, in whole or in part, in Lord Dufferin, *Irish Emigration and the Tenure of Land in Ireland* (London, 1867); Frederic Seebohm, *The English Village Community* (London, 1883); H. L. Gray, *English Field Systems* (Cambridge Mass., 1915).
18. *Report on Destitution*, p. 48.
19. Evans, *Geography*, 24 (1939), 35.
20. *Digest of Evidence*, Part II (1848), pp. 420, 423.
21. *Report on Destitution*, p. 18.
22. *Ibid.*, p. 398.
23. *Ibid.*, Introduction.
24. *Dublin University Magazine*, 51 (1858), 731–41.
25. *Report on Destitution*, Introduction.
26. *Ibid.*, p. 361.
27. This was Lord George's view. It is an open question how far an apparent disregard for material comfort in housing and clothing is to be regarded as an old cultural feature of peasant society in Ireland. Many writers have explained it as a defensive mechanism against rackrenting landlords.
28. Sir Henry Robinson, *Memories: Wise and Otherwise* (London, 1924), p. 49.
29. *Digest of Evidence*, Part I (1947), p. 294.
30. H.F. Hore, 'The Archaeology of Ulster Tenant Right', *Ulster J. Archaeol.* 1st S., 6 (1858), 109–25.
31. *Report on Destitution*, p. 42.
32. J.R. Fox, 'Kinship and Land Tenure on Tory Island', *Ulster Folklife*, 12 (1966), 1–17.
33. D. McCourt, 'The Cruck Truss in Ireland and its west European Connexions', *Folkliv*, 28/29 (1964–5), 64–78.
34. A. Gailey, 'Irish Corn-drying kilns', *Ulster Folklife*, 15/16 (1970), 52–71. Two such kilns are marked on fig. 11.

Bibliography

F.H.A. Aalen, 'The Origins of Enclosures in eastern Ireland', in Stephens and Glasscock (eds.), *Irish Geographical Studies* (1970).

B. Adams, 'Language and Man in Ireland', *Ulster Folklife*, 15/16 (1970), 140–71.

G.B. Adams (ed.), *Ulster Dialects* (Ulster Folk Museum, 1964).

E.C. Amoroso and P.A. Jewell, 'The exploitation of the milk-ejection reflex by primitive peoples', in Mourant and Zeuner (eds.), *Man and Cattle* (Roy. Anthrop. Inst., 1963).

J.H. Andrews, 'Geography and Government in Elizabethan Ireland', in Stephens and Glasscock (eds.), *Irish Geographical Studies* (1970).

A. ApSimon, 'The earlies Bronze Age in the North of Ireland', *Ulster J. Archaeol.* 32 (1970), 28–72.

C.M. Arensberg, *The Irish Countryman* (London, 1937).

C.M. Arensberg and S.T. Kimball, *Family and Community in Ireland* (Cambridge Mass., 1940).

J.C. Beckett, *The Study of Irish History*, Inaugural Lecture (Belfast, 1963).

J.C. Beckett, *The Making of Modern Ireland 1603–1923* (London, 1966).

J. Beddoe, *The Races of Britain* (London, 1885; reprinted 1971).

M. Beresford, *The Lost Villages of England* (London, 1954).

D.A. Binchy, 'The Linguistic and Historical value of the Irish Law Tracts', *Proc. Brit. Acad.* 29 (1943), 195–227.

D.A. Binchy, 'Secular Institutions', in Dillon (ed.), *Early Irish Society* (1954).

M. Bloch, *Les Caractères Originaux de l'Histoire rurale française* (Oslo, 1931; London, 1966).

M. Bloch, *Feudal Society*, translated by L.A. Manyon (London, 1961).

E.G. Bowen, *Saints, Seaways and Settlements in the Celtic Lands* (Cardiff, 1969).

F. Braudel, *La Mediterranée et le monde mediterranéen à l'Epoque de Philippe II* (Paris, 1949).

R.H. Buchanan, 'Common fields and enclosure: an eighteenth century example from Lecale, County Down', *Ulster Folklife*, 15/16 (1970), 99–118.

R.H. Buchanan, 'Rural Settlement in Ireland', in Stephens and Glasscock (eds.), *Irish Geographical Studies* (1970).

R.H. Buchanan, E. Jones and D. McCourt (eds.), *Man and his Habitat* (London, 1971).

R.A. Butlin, 'Urban Genesis in Ireland, 1556–1641', in Steel and Lawton (eds.), *Liverpool Essays in Geography* (London, 1967).

A. Campbell, 'Irish Fields and Houses', *Béaloideas*, 5 (1935), 57–74.

A. Campbell, 'Notes on the Irish House', *Folkliv* (1937), 207–34; (1938), 173–96.

H. Case, 'Settlement-patterns in the north Irish Neolithic', *Ulster J. Archaeol.* 32 (1969), 3–27.

V.G. Childe, *What Happened in History* (Harmondsworth, 1942).

T. Colby, *Memoir of the City and North Western Liberties of Londonderry* (Dublin, 1837).

G.A.J. Cole, *Ireland the Outpost* (Oxford, 1919).

J.M. Coles, 'Some Irish Horns of the late Bronze Age', *J. Roy. Soc. Antiq. Ireland*, 97 (1967), 113–17.

R.G. Collingwood, *The Idea of History* (Oxford, 1946).

K.H. Connell, *The Population of Ireland, 1750–1845* (Oxford, 1950).

K.H. Connell, *Irish Peasant Society* (Oxford, 1968).

C.S. Coon, *The Races of Europe* (New York, 1939).

M. Craig, *The Personality of Leinster* (Dublin, 1961; reprinted 1971).

G.L. Davies, 'The enigma of the Irish Tertiary', in Stephens and Glasscock (eds.), *Irish Geographical Studies* (1970).
H.C. Darby (ed.), *The Domesday Geography of England* (Cambridge, 1952–71).
H.C. Darby, 'On the Relations of Geography and History', in Dohrs and Sommers (eds.), *Cultural Geography: Selected Readings* (New York, 1967).
P. Vidal de la Blache, *Tableau de la Géographie de la France* (Paris, 1911).
M. and L. de Paor, *Early Christian Ireland* (London, 1958).
X. de Planhol, 'Le Chien de Berger', *Bull. de l'Assoc. de Géographes français*, 370 (1969), 355–68.
R. de Valera, 'The Court Cairns of Ireland', *Proc. Roy. Irish Acad.* 60 (1960), 9–140.
M. Dillon, The Archaism of Celtic Tradition, *Proc. Brit. Acad.* 53 (1947), 345–64.
M. Dillon (ed.), *Early Irish Society* (Dublin, 1954).
M. Dillon and N. Chadwick, *The Celtic Realms* (London, 1967).
F.E. Dohrs and L.M. Sommers (eds.), *Cultural Geography: Selected Readings* (New York, 1967).
M. Duignan, 'Irish agriculture in early historic times', *J. Roy. Soc. Antiq. Ireland*, 74 (1944), 1–22.
L. Durrell, *The Spirit of Place* (London, 1969).
J. Dutton, letter written c. 1700, *Analecta Hibernica*, 2 (1931), 51.
S. Erixon, 'West European connections and culture relations', *Folkliv* (1938), 137–72.
E.E. Evans, 'Some Survivals of the Irish openfield system', *Geography*, 24 (1939), 24–36.
E.E. Evans, *Irish Heritage: the landscape, the people and their work* (Dundalk, 1942).
E.E. Evans, *Mourne Country: landscape and life in south Down* (Dundalk, 1951).
E.E. Evans, *Irish Folk Ways* (London, 1957).
E.E. Evans, 'The Atlantic Ends of Europe', *Adv. Science*, 15 (1958), 54–64.
E.E. Evans, 'The Peasant and the Past', *Adv. Science*, 17 (1960), 293–302.
E.E. Evans, *Prehistoric and Early Christian Ireland: A guide* (London, 1966).
E.E. Evans, 'Donegal Harvest', *Ulster Folklife*, 14 (1968), 3–5.
E.E. Evans, 'The Personality of Ulster', *Trans. Inst. Brit. Geographers*, 51 (1970), 1–20.
E.E. Evans, Introduction to Gailey and Fenton (eds.), *The Spade in Northern and Atlantic Europe* (1970).
E.E. Evans, Introduction to Hill, *Facts from Gweedore* (Belfast, 1971).
L. Febvre, *La Terre et l'Evolution humaine* (Paris, 1922).
W. Fitzgerald, *The Historical Geography of early Ireland* (London, 1925).
P. Flatrès, *Géographie rurale de quatre contrées Celtiques* (Rennes, 1957).
H.J. Fleure, *The Trilogy of the humanities in education* (Aberystwyth, 1918).
H.J. Fleure, 'Archaeology and Folk Tradition', *Proc. Brit. Acad.* 17 (1931), 3–24.
H.J. Fleure, 'Prehistoric elements in our heritage', *Bull. John Rylands Lib.* 18 (1934), 3–36.
H.J. Fleure, 'Folk-lore and Culture-contacts', *Bull. John Rylands Lib.* 23 (1939), 1–14.
H.J. Fleure, Introduction to Vidal de la Blache, *La Personnalité géographique de la France* (Manchester, 1941).
H.J. Fleure and M. Davies, *A Natural History of Man in Britain* (London, 1971).
R. Flower, *The Irish Tradition* (Oxford, 1947).
A.C. Forbes, 'Some legendary and historical references to Irish woods and their significance', *Proc. Roy. Irish Acad.* 41 (1932), 15–36.
Sir Cyril Fox, *The Personality of Britain* (Cardiff, 1932).
T.W. Freeman, *Ireland: Its physical, historical and economic geography* (London, 1950; 4th ed., 1969).
T.W. Freeman, *Pre-Famine Ireland: a study in historical geography* (London, 1957).
O.H. Frey (ed.), *Festschrift Dehn* (Bonn, 1969).
A. Gailey and A. Fenton (eds.), *The Spade in Northern and Atlantic Europe* (Ulster Folk Museum, 1970).

A. Gailey, 'The Typology of the Irish Spade', in Gailey and Fenton (eds.), *The Spade in Northern and Atlantic Europe* (1970).

Gaeltacht Studies, vol. 1: A Development Plan for the Gaeltacht (Dublin, 1971).

M.J. Gardiner and P. Ryan, 'A new generalised Soil Map of Ireland, and its land-use interpretation', *Irish J. Agric. Research*, 8 (1969), 95–109.

C.T. Glacken, *Traces on the Rhodian Shore: Nature and culture in western thought from ancient times to the end of the eighteenth century* (Berkeley, 1967).

R. Glasscock, 'Moated sites and deserted boroughs and villages: two neglected aspects of Anglo-Norman settlement in Ireland', in Stephens and Glasscock (eds.), *Irish Geographical Studies* (1970).

Y. Goblet, *La Transformation de la Géographie politique de l'Irlande au XVIIe siècle*, 2 vols. (Paris, 1930).

J. Graham, 'Transhumance in Ireland', *Adv. Science*, 37 (1953), 74–9.

J. Graham, 'Rural Society in Connacht, 1600–1640', in Stephens and Glasscock (eds.), *Irish Geographical Studies* (1970).

H.L. Gray, *English Field Systems*, (Cambridge Mass., 1915).

J.R. Green, *The Making of England* (London, 1881).

D. Greene, 'Early Irish Literature', in Dillon (ed.), *Early Irish Society* (1954).

D. Greene, *The Irish Language* (Dublin, 1966).

E. Hackett and M.E. Folan, 'The ABO and RH Blood Groups of the Aran Islands', *Irish J. Medical Science*, 390 (1958), 247–61.

P. Harbinson, 'Catalogue of Irish early Bronze Age associated finds containing Copper and Bronze', *Proc. Roy. Irish Acad.* 67 (1968), 35–91.

P. Harbinson, *Die Prähistorische Bronzefunde Europas*, 6, 1. (*The Axes of the early Bronze Age in Ireland*) (Munich, 1969).

P. Harbinson, 'The Chariot of Celtic funerary tradition', in Frey (ed.), *Festschrift Dehn* (Bonn, 1969).

G.A. Hayes-McCoy, *Scots Mercenary Forces in Ireland, 1565–1603* (London, 1937).

G.A. Hayes-McCoy, 'Gaelic Society in Ireland in the late sixteenth century', *Historical Studies*, 4 (1963), 45–61.

P.L. Henry, 'Anglo-Irish Word-charts', in Adams (ed.), *Ulster Dialects* (Ulster Folk Museum, 1964),

M. Herity, 'Prehistoric fields in Ireland', *Irish University Review* (Spring, 1971), 258–61.

M.W. Heslinga, *The Irish Border as a cultural divide* (Assen, 1962; reprinted 1971).

Lord George Hill, *Facts from Gweedore* (London, 1845; Belfast, 1971).

A.E. Hooton and C.W. Dupertuis, *The Physical Anthropology of Ireland* (Cambridge Mass., 1955).

T. Jones Hughes, 'Society and settlement in 19th century Ireland', *Irish Geography*, 5 (1965), 79–96.

T. Jones Hughes, 'Town and Baile in Irish Place-names', in Stephens and Glasscock (eds.), Irish Geographical Studies (1970).

K. Hughes, *The Church in early Irish Society* (London, 1966).

E. Huntington, *Civilization and Climate* (New Haven, 1915).

J. Huxley, in Wolstenholme (ed.), *Man and his Future* (London, 1963).

K. Jackson, *The oldest Irish Tradition: a window on the Iron Age* (Cambridge, 1964).

G. Jenkins (ed.), *Studies in Folk Life* (London 1969).

J.H. Johnson, 'The two "Irelands" at the beginning of the 19th century', in Stephens and Glasscock (eds.), *Irish Geographical Studies* (1970).

E. Jones, *The Social Geography of Belfast* (London, 1960).

F.P. Jones, 'The Gwerin of Wales', in Jenkins (ed.), *Studies in Folk Life* (London, 1969).

G. Jones, 'The Multiple Estate as a model framework for tracing the early stages in the evolution of early settlement', in *L'Habitat et les Paysages ruraux d'Europe* (Liége, 1971).

P. Kavanagh, *The Green Fool* (London, 1938).

J. Kelleher, 'Early Irish history and pseudo-history', *Studia Hibernica*, 3 (1963), pp. 113–27.

F.R. Leavis and D. Thompson, *Culture and Environment* (London, 1937).

J. Leighley (ed.), *Landscape and Life: a selection from the writings of Carl Ortwin Sauer* (Berkeley (1965).

D. Linton, 'Tertiary landscape evolution', in Watson and Sissons (eds.), *The British Isles* (Edinburgh, 1964).

A. Lomax, *Folk Song Style and Culture* (Amer. Ass. Adv. Science, 1969).

A.T. Lucas, 'The plundering and burning of Churches in Ireland, 7th to 16th century', in Rynne (ed.), *North Munster Studies* (Limerick, 1967).

F.S. Lyons, *Ireland since the Famine* (London, 1971).

R.A.S. Macalister, *Ancient Ireland* (London, 1935).

P. MacCana, *Celtic Mythology* (London, 1970).

Sir H.J. Mackinder, *Britain and the British Seas* (Oxford, 1906; 2nd ed. 1922).

E. MacNeill, *Early Irish Laws and Institutions* (Dublin, 1935).

M. MacNeill, *The Festival of Lughnasa* (London, 1962).

F.W. Maitland, *Domesday Book and Beyond* (Cambridge, 1907).

D. McCourt, 'Infield and Outfield in Ireland', *Econ. Hist. Rev.* 7 (1954–5), 369–76.

D. McCourt, 'The dynamic quality of Irish rural settlement,' in Buchanan *et al.* (eds.), *Man and his Habitat* (1971).

E. McCracken, *The Irish woods since Tudor times: their distribution and exploitation* (Newton Abbot, 1971).

J. McEvoy, *Statistical Survey of the county of Tyrone* (Dublin, 1802).

A. Meitzen, *Siedelung und Agrarwesen*, 3 vols. and atlas (Berlin, 1895).

J. C. Messenger, *Inis Beag: Isle of Ireland* (New York, 1969).

G.F. Mitchell, 'Post-boreal pollen diagrams from Irish raised-bogs', *Proc. Roy. Irish Acad.* 57 (1956), 185–252.

J.M. Mogey, *Rural life in Northern Ireland* (London, 1947).

T.W. Moody, 'A New History of Ireland', *Irish Historical Studies*, 16 (1969), 1–17.

T.W. Moody, and F.X. Martin (eds.), *The Course of Irish History* (Cork, 1967).

A.E. Mourant and F.E. Zeuner (eds.), *Man and Cattle* (Roy. Anthrop. Inst., 1963).

A. Nicholson, *Ireland's Welcome to the Stranger* (London, 1847).

E.R. Norman and J.K. St Joseph, *The Early Development of Irish Society* (Cambridge, 1969).

E. O'Curry and W.K. Sullivan, *Manners and Customs of the ancient Irish*, 3 vols. (Dublin, 1873).

C. O Danachair, 'Three house types', *Ulster Folklife*, 2 (1956), 22–6.

C. O Danachair, 'Some distribution patterns in Irish Folklife', *Béaloideas*, 24 (1957), 108–23.

C. O Danachair, 'The use of the spade in Ireland', in Gailey and Fenton (eds.), *The Spade in Northern and Atlantic Europe* (1970).

M.J. O'Kelly, 'Excavations and experiments in ancient Irish cooking-places', *J. Roy. Soc. Antiq. Ireland*, 84 (1954), 105–55.

J.J. O'Meara, *The Topography of Ireland by Giraldus Cambrensis* (Dundalk, 1951).

S. O Nualláin and R. de Valera, *Survey of the Megalithic tombs of Ireland*, vol. 1, *County Clare* (Dublin, 1961).

S.P. O'Riordain, 'Lough Gur excavations', *Proc. Roy. Irish Acad.* 56 (1954).

A. Orme, *Ireland* (The World's Landscapes, 4) (London, 1970).

S. O Súilleabháin, *A Handbook of Irish Folklore* (Dublin, 1942).

S. O Súilleabháin, *Irish Wake Amusements* (Cork, 1967).

A.J. Otway-Ruthven, 'The organisation of Anglo-Norman agriculture in the Middle Ages', *J. Roy. Soc. Antiq. Ireland*, 81 (1951), 1–13.

H.J.E. Peake and H.J. Fleure, *The Corridors of Time*, 10 vols. (Oxford, 1927–56).

W.J. Perry, *The Growth of Civilisation* (London, 1924).

S. Piggott, 'Ireland and Britain in Prehistory: Changing viewpoints and perspective', *J. Cork Hist. and Archaeol. Soc.* 71 (1966), 5–18.

T.G.E. Powell, *The Celts* (London, 1958).

V.B. Proudfoot, 'Clachans in Ireland', *Gwerin*, 2 (1959), 110–22.

D.B. Quinn, 'Sir Thomas Smith (1513–77) and the beginnings of English colonial theory', *Proc. Amer. Philosoph. Soc.* 89 (1945), 544–60.

D.B. Quinn, *The Elizabethans and the Irish* (Ithaca, 1966).

J. Raftery (ed.), *The Celts* (Cork, 1964).

Lord Raglan, *How came Civilisation?* (London, 1939).

A. Ross, *Pagan Celtic Britain* (London, 1967).

J. Ryan, *Irish Monasticism* (Dublin, 1931).

J. Ryan (ed.), *Saint Patrick* (Dublin, 1958).

E. Rynne (ed.), *North Munster Studies* (Limerick, 1967).

R.N. Salaman, *The history and social influence of the potato* (Cambridge, 1949).

C.O. Sauer, 'The Personality of Mexico', in Leighley (ed.), *Landscape and Life: a selection from the writings of Carl Ortwin Sauer* (Berkeley, 1965).

A. Smith, 'Late- and post-glacial vegetational and climatic history of Ireland', in Stephens and Glasscock (eds.), *Irish Geographical Studies* (1970).

G.E. Smith, *The Diffusion of Culture* (London, 1933).

O.H.K. Spate, 'Reflections on A Study of History', in *Let me Enjoy* (Canberra, 1965).

R.W. Steel and R. Lawton (eds.), *Liverpool Essays in Geography* (London, 1967).

N. Stephens and R.E. Glasscock (eds.), *Irish Geographical Studies* (Belfast, 1970).

W. Stokes, *The Life of George Petrie* (London, 1868).

M. Tierney (ed.), *Daniel O'Connell: nine centenary essays* (Dublin, 1945).

H. Uhlig, 'Old hamlets with infield and outfield systems in western and central Europe', *Geografiska Annaler*, 43 (1961), 285–312.

H. Wagner, 'The Origin of the Celts in the light of linguistic geography', *Philolog. Trans.* (1969), 203–50.

J.M. Watson and S.B. Sissons (eds.), *The British Isles* (Edinburgh, 1964).

G. Wolstenholme (ed.), *Man and his Future* (London, 1963).

F. Young, *Ireland at the Crossroads* (London, 1903).

Index

Acton, Lord, 5
Adams, Brendan, 45f
Ahoghill, Co. Antrim, 74
Alcoholism, 38, 46, 107 n.20
Anglo-Irish literature, 3, 83
Anglo-Norman, 14, 35, 52, 55–8, 73
Annals, Irish, 52, 76f
Anthropogeography, 1, 46f
Anthropology, academic, 4
Antrim, Co., 24, 71
Araire, see Plough
Aran Is., 44, 83
Archaeology, academic, 3
Armagh, 75
Armagh, Co., 30
Arranmore I., Co. Donegal, 89
Athlone, Co. Westmeath, 25
Atlantic climate, 33
Atlantic edge, 19 fig. 1, 20
Atlantic Europe, 7, 12, 18, 20, 60, 65, 70, 109 n.46.

Ballyarr, Co. Donegal, 87
Ballyglass, Co. Mayo, 61, 64
Ballynagilly, Co. Tyrone, 64
Bann, River, 35, 69
Barker, Sir E., 67
Beakers, 49
Beckett, J.C., 15, 16
Beddoe, J., 69
Beech, 32, 68
Belfast, 3, 4, 25, 68, 82, 85
Beltany Mt., Co. Donegal, 90
Beltany Upper, 96, 97, 98–9 figs. 11–14
Benbulbin, Co. Sligo, 24
Beresford, M., 13
Betaghs, 56, 58
Binchy, D.A., 34, 57, 73
Black Pig's Dyke, 28
Bloch, Marc, 6, 10, 15, 53, 67, 72, 84
Blood groups, 44
Bloody Foreland, Co. Donegal, 85, 88, 104
Bogs, basin, 31, 35
Bogs, blanket, 26, 35f, 41, 61, 85, 88
Booleying, 61, 79f, 85, 90. *See also* Transhumance
Boreal climate, 35
Borrow, George, 52
Bowen, E.G., 75

Boyne culture, 29, 72
Boyne, River, 23, 31, 41, 45, 47ff, 72
Braudel, F., 10, 15, 17, 79
Bronze Age, 33, 43, 48ff, 61, 69, 89f
Brown earths, 39, 67
Buchail, 80
Bunbeg, Co. Donegal, 88, 104
Burren, the, Co. Clare, 24, 79
Burtonport, Co. Donegal, 88

Campbell, A., 63
Carbon dating, 4, 42, 71
Carlyle T., 87
Carrownaglogh, Co. Mayo, 61, pl. 1*b*
Caulfield, S., 61
Cavan, Co., 30, 31
Celtic art, 46, 72, 78
Celtic Christianity, 16, 20, 75f
Celtic languages, 6, 44f, 48. *See also* Gaelic language
Celtic race, 43, 45, 108 n.5
Central Lowlands, 24–7, 29, 31
Chariot, 50
Childe, V.G., 5, 6, 9
Clachan, 55, 56 fig. 9, 58, 60f, 81, 89, pl. 3
Clady River, Co. Donegal, 88, 104
Clare, Co., 24, 74, 79
Clare Island, Co. Mayo, pl. 1*a*
Clark, Grahame, 5
Classical geography, 2, 4, 7
Clew Bay, Co. Mayo, 31
Climate, 6f, 12, 32ff
Climatic deterioration, 6f, 33f, 41
Cloghaneely, Co. Donegal, 88, 101
Colby, T., 78
Cole, G., 18, 26
Collingwood, R.G., 4
Congested Districts Board, 95, 103
Connacht, 20, 29, 59f, 63, 74, 79, 104
Connell, K. H., 13
Connemara, 21, 69
Cork, Co., 49
Court graves, *see* Graves
Craig, Sir J., 80
Crannog, *see* Lake-dwelling
Crawford, O.G.S., 7
Creaght, 80
Cricket, 53
Croagh Patrick, Co. Mayo, 48, 75f.

119